# *Marriage Advice self-help books*

## *THIS BOOK INCLUDES:*

### *Communication in Marriage Workbook*

### *And*

### *Marriage Counseling Workbook*

© written by: Katerina Griffith

# *Communication in Marriage Workbook*

*Your ultimate Guide to a non-violent Relationship that Thrives on Effective Communication Skills in Marriage*

## Table of Contents

# *The Marriage Counseling Workbook*

## *Guide to Effective Marriage Therapy and Communication Techniques for a Healthy and Long- Lasting Relationship*

# Book Description

Falling in love with your spouse for the very first time was all consuming, right? Well, maintaining that love and affection takes more effort.

Do you compliment your spouse's physical appearances anymore? Do you feel that rush in adrenaline when your spouse walks into the room? How often do you hold each other's hands? What happened to all the flirting, sex and orgasms? What happened to the heightened level of foreplay sexuality and true sensuality?

Everything revolves around communication!

It is not that communication techniques are inherently flawed. Think of it as having better diet tips where you eat less and move more. In the same manner, communication is not about words, it is about emotional states. Research shows that we make judgments of what someone says based on their emotional tone: facial expressions, level of distractedness, body language, tone of voice, and eye contact.

What is your gut feeling when your partner uses "communication techniques" on you? Does it feel respectful or patronizing? In this book, we will delve deeper into;

- How to get your partner do or stop doing something
- Ways you can express yourself to be heard by your spouse
- Justifying your negative feelings
- Rekindling the spark and intimacy in your marriage

This book will definitely streamline your communication and snap you out of la-la land so that you can focus on every detail of your marriage experience.

So, what are you still waiting for? It's time to spice things up, upgrade your sex positions, get random and have all the mind-blowing sex that lights a fire in your heart, gut and awakens the sexy beast in you.

Come with me!

# Introduction

One very important aspect of life is communication. In marriage, a small communication breakdown can bring the whole union down. It can destroy several years of work. It is this very reason that as a couple, you have to pay attention to your communication with your partner or spouse.

Well, easier said than done, right?

According to Jonathan Robinson, a couple's therapist, communication is critical in ensuring that your partner feels understood and their emotions are valued. When this does not happen, relationships and marriages begin to have problems. In a divorce session, you never hear couples say that we understood each other perfectly well and that is why we want a divorce, do we?

The truth is that, no one is born a natural communicator. Just like riding a bicycle, communication is a skill that one has to learn. And the only way you are going to improve your relationship is by ensuring that you foster good communication.

My best friend's parents fought with each other every single night until they divorced when we were in 7th grade. You may have faced the same thing in your family, marriage or neighborhood. You may even know couples who hardly talked to each other at all and ended up in divorce. This may make you question whether it is possible to even have a stable marriage at all.

Where do you look when your parents or guardians were not good role models of communication in marriage?

Here, we will offer deeper insight into how you can make your marriage loving. One thing that you need to bear in mind is that communication in marriage is a like a river. When you allow your thoughts and emotions to flow smoothly between the two of you. This is exactly what makes your marriage fun and supports everything that you do together.

However, when your communication flow is turbulent, it can be potentially dangerous and destructive. When there is blockage, this tends to stir up pressure and when words begin to flow, they come off in a rather damaging rage.

You will note that couples often try to evade having difficult conversations in marriage and this affects the health of their marriage. You find yourself going back and forth about who is supposed to pick the kids from school, who will pay the bills, who will run a certain errand, or go where and when without really delving deeper into conversations that are important to you. With time, this kind of communication sucks all the passion and love you have with each other and what is left is a sour relationship.

You may ask, but what does a great communication in marriage even look like? Well, we will discuss this in more details later in the book. However, one thing that you need to note is that a great relationship is one in which couples talk openly and freely with one another while feeling safe whenever they share private thoughts. It is about verbalizing all your concerns and emotions whenever they arise. It is about voicing all your positive thoughts when good things happen.

Having a great communication is about being tactful and keeping off attacks, hurtful and condescending comments. You are required to ensure that you pay attention to what your spouse is saying, so that you can understand where they are coming from and express sympathy rather than always digging to find what is wrong in what they say or even

14

dismissing what you hear. Irrespective of what your partner's perspective is, you both feel good after having a conversation with each other. You feel that your concerns have been put into consideration and are being addressed.

Trust me, all these takes a lot of effort learning. It takes lots of practice to perfect. And most important, it takes a great teacher that can truly demonstrate to you how you can do it right.

# Chapter 1
# Basics of good communication in marriage

## *What is communication?*

This is one of the questions that everyone has a unique answer for. But generally, communication can be defined as the process by which you send information and receive a message whether verbally or non-verbally.

So, you meet a friend on the way and you wave at them, that is a form of communication. You write a graphical representation of a school project you are working on, that is a form of communication. You blow a kiss at your lover, that is a form of communication. Therefore, think of communication as a way in which you create and exchange meaning.

According to James Carey, a media critic and theorist, communication is a process that is rather symbolic and it entails production, maintenance, repair and transformation of the reality. It is the manner in which we share our realities and experiences with others.

Every creature on earth has developed a means of conveying thoughts and emotional feelings to each other. However, what makes the human race quite unique is the fact that we can use both words and language to transfer meaning.

*What is the concept of communication?*

To break things down, let's imagine communication in the form of sending, receiving and interpreting the meaning of a message on both ends. In other words, when you transmit a message, the receiver on the other hand will give you feedback. Therefore, communication is happening both during conveyance of the message and afterwards. The signals that you can use to give feedback can either be verbal or non-verbal. For instance, you can nod your head to show that you agree with what is being said.

The other concept is the context of the message, the surrounding it is given in, and potential for interference during transmission and reception.

If you can see the sender when receiving a message, you will not only have access to the content of the message, but also the nonverbal communication the sender conveys. You can tell whether the sender is nervous or professional. If as a receiver you can hear the sender, then you are better placed to pick cues from their tone as well.

### Rhetorical communication

This is also referred to as the written form of communication. This is one other thing that sets humanity apart from other creatures. This is one other way in which you can communicate your thoughts and feelings to the other party. Well, the fact that there are so many forms of communication simply means that there even more ways to be misunderstood.

When communicating with your partner through written forms such as emails, text message, twitter, WhatsApp chat among others, it is critical that you stay clear in what you are writing and how you structure the message to avoid misinterpretation. You may write an email that is interpreted as cold or clipped, something that you did not intend from the very beginning.

### Types of communication in marriage

### Verbal communication

We all like to hear people complement our looks. We also like to hear that we are loved and respected. Verbal communication refers to your ability to express by way of words how you feel about something. This is a very essential form of communication in marriage.

If you love your spouse with the whole of your heart and yet fail to say it, the truth is that your spouse will not understand how deeply you love them. Yes, you may appreciate your spouse but if you never speak about it, that appreciation does not hold much value. On the other hand, if you tell your spouse how wonderful they are, they will definitely feel appreciated and will be in touch with just how you feel about them deep inside.

Just as you express how much pleasure you feel about your spouse, it is important that you also let them know what you are not happy about. Communicating effectively in marriage is what determines your marital bliss. If your partner keeps doing something that you do not like, tell them. When you remain silent about the things that bother you, you are not only letting them continue with the action, but also are allowing your trust chip away little by little.

Trust me, the last thing you want is going through life with your spouse holding on to all the dissatisfactions you have about them deep inside your heart. It is critical that you let it all out so that your relationship is healed and stays healthy. That said, you have to do it in a tactful and warm manner so that it is not too late to say it when you have had plenty of room to say what you have in your heart. Truth is, if verbal communication is not effective in your marriage, this can take a toll on your mental health.

*Nonverbal communication*

Have you ever said something to your spouse that was met with an unexpected facial expression? Truth is, your spouse did not have to say a word for you to know what they felt. Their facial expression told the whole story. Well, nonverbal communication is not just about facial expressions, it is what we speak in many other ways other than written or spoken word.

As we talk about how communication is important in marriage, the truth is that we cannot underplay how paramount nonverbal cues are. When having a conversation with your partner, it is important that you stay aware of how your body language communicates with your partner. Ask yourself whether you are hunched over or closed off while having an important conversation. Chances are that your partner will sense that lack of vulnerability.

Start by facing your husband or wife and ensure that your body language is open when having a difficult discussion. Do not clench your fist, cross your legs, fidget, or cross your arms. It is critical that your body tells your spouse that you are open to hearing what they have to say and have the willingness to work through it.

That said, there are so many nonverbal cues that are quite similar to being closed off and communicates either positive or negative information to your partner without necessarily exchanging words. Ensure that you are not only thoughtful but also conscious about what your language speaks of your feelings/emotions. It is through proper nonverbal communication that you can de-escalate several conflicting situations.

*Physical acts*

Taking out the garbage, making dinner, picking the kids from school, dropping the kids to school, going grocery shopping, and running for ice cream at the store for your pregnant wife are all examples of physical acts. These are not things that you say. Instead, they are things you do to express to your spouse that you care so much about them.

When you do these small and thoughtful acts, you are expressing your love for your significant other without saying much at all. This form of communication is great for those who are not great with the verbal form of communication. This is where the phrase "actions speak louder than words" come in to play.

Trust me, there is a huge difference between telling your wife or husband that you love them and showing it by doing some of the house chores like cleaning, or even changing the oil in her car. Physical acts tend to resonate with your partner much more than words. They have a lasting effect. You may shower your husband with so much compliments but making his favorite meal will do the trick all day every day.

Importance of communication in marriage is something that cannot be emphasized enough. It is by employing open channels of communication that you ensure less misunderstandings arise so that you can strengthen your marriage in a well-rounded manner.

If your marriage is going to be successful, then the very first thing is for you to ensure that you apply a combination of all the forms we have discussed above. This way, you will stroke a good balance that will tell your spouse just how much they mean to you.

Tell them how you love them and what it is that you love most about them. Do not be afraid to let them know your thoughts and emotional feelings even if they are worrying and uncomfortable. It is through open and honest communication that will hold your marriage together for years to come.

It is critical that your spouse knows that you are being honest and open by just examining your body language. When you close yourself off, cover your mouth, mumble words and make negative facial expressions, you are sending them red flags. When you stay conscious of your body language and make proper adjustments, you are simply telling your spouse that you are being genuine and that they can trust you.

Do not hesitate. Use actions to communicate your honesty, love and trust with your spouse. Give them that massage their body has been dying for, buy them a thoughtful gift on your way home, help them with tasks that have been giving them sleepless nights. Truth is, words do not have to be spoken because actions will speak for themselves!

What happens before hitting the "send" button?

Well, when preparing a message to be send either verbally through the phone or written in an email, it is critical that you think of the person that is going to receive it on the other end. Think about the information you intend to share, the context and the means of conveying it. Ask yourself whether the means you have selected is the most effective one or not. Is there something more you can do to ensure that your message is conveyed correctly?

Sending a message to your spouse is quite different from when you are sending it for a professional audience. Ensure that the language used is right.

Now, let us play a small game. Imagine yourself out in the public asking people (strangers) what they think about marriage. What do you think they would say in just one word?

Chances are that you will hear words like Love, Trust, Respect, and Honesty among others. And yes, all these are very essential components of a marriage. Ironically, the one factor that is fundamentally important and yet less talked about is *communication*.

The manner in which a couple discusses their issues, if they discuss at all, is critical in determining whether a marriage is self-sustaining and fulfilling. Still wondering why communication is important in marriage? Read on.

# Chapter 2
# The magic of communication in marriage

It is quite unfortunate that the importance of communication is often not taken seriously in marriage. This is mainly because so many couples think daily banter or lack thereof does not affect them every day.

However, you must understand that communication is the engine that fuels all other parts of a marriage. If you love your spouse and fail to show them through words and actions, then the truth is that you are not doing right by them. If you genuinely love and trust them, then let them know how you feel about them. Communicating openly and with honesty ensures that your marriage stands a chance of flourishing and staying healthy. Communication must begin right from the time you are courting to marriage and into marriage.

When you and your husband or wife make effective communication the cornerstone of your marriage, you will enjoy a loving marriage. The only shortcoming is that there are people who are just not good at it. Having love, honesty, and trust is good, but they are not meaningful by themselves. It is by expressing these traits that yield a marriage that will become the envy of many.

The magic lies in **showing** love, **acting** honestly, and **showcasing** trust. Communicating how much your husband or wife means to you moves your marriage from good to high! The point is, expressing yourself goes beyond words alone.

Some of the benefits associated with effective communication in marriage include;

### Minimizing confusion

Did you know that when you have been married to someone for 50+ years, you still cannot predict what is going through their mind? One of the biggest mistakes that couples today make is assuming that their spouse "knows." The problem with this kind of assumption is that your spouse may be thinking a complete opposite of what you thought at first.

According to Eboni Baugh and Deborah Humphreys (Extension specialists at the

University of Florida), it is critical that you clearly state your thoughts with utmost honesty to minimize confusion. Additionally, when saying your thoughts, do it positively as much as you can.

When you minimize confusion, what you are doing is increasing the commitment in your relationship. This commitment is what is directly related to satisfaction in marriage.

### *It maintains marriages through assurances*

Satisfaction in relationships is directly correlated to the assurance that you give your partner. Marianne Dainton, a communications researcher, explains that assurance in marriage is what reaffirms you're the romantic desires of your partner. You can achieve this by choosing to use kind words and acts of love.

Other researchers report that couples who often engage in assurances often enjoy more significant commitment in their marriage which impacts positively on their marital satisfaction.

### *Enhances marital satisfaction*

As we have already discussed, it is evident that

when communications are effective in marriage, then couples can enjoy marital satisfaction. When you are satisfied in marriage, you will live a healthier life, and this will increase your lifespan significantly.

However, if you are in a marriage that is characterized by poor communications, you will likely be caught up in a vicious cycle of poor, unhealthy conversations that contribute to dissatisfaction. When this cycle of poor communication is not corrected early enough, it has a likelihood of degrading your relationship.

### *Keeps a couple closer than they think*

How do you know your spouse for who they are? Is there a way to know? One thing that you need to bear in mind is that no one has a premonition or the power to read other's minds. When we share our life's stories and experiences, we are certainly going to involve ourselves with others.

The same thing applies to marriage. Marriage is not just about physical contact; it is also about having an emotional connection with another. When you share a little experience from your life with someone however small it may be, this form of openness will surely draws you nearer to one another. It is what makes you both feel like one.

29

The only way you are going to know what is going through your spouse's mind and heart is by asking them. This is one of the best ways to resolve any issues that arise in a fast and effective way possible.

## Assumptions and misunderstandings are likely not to creep in

One of the things that we have mentioned earlier is that of making assumptions. But the most critical question is, how does communication in marriage ensure that assumptions and misunderstanding do not creep in?

Well, one thing that we have to note is that it is natural for one's mind to wander off and have the worst thoughts possible when they feel that their spouse is not sharing some specific information.

Think about a situation where you and your significant other speak to each other without any inhibitions. Will there be any form of negativity? Certainly not! The main reason is that you are ensuring that you close the door for assumptions. This way, you eliminate negativity out of your life.

Once you know what you both like and dislike

beliefs, desires, opinions, and wants in life, you both will likely decide to see your marriage through to success. But the question is, "what do you think is holding you back?" Well, when you open your heart to someone else, this is indeed a blessing. The main reason is that you know that there is someone in this life that knows and appreciates you for who you truly are.

Therefore, ensure that you are not keeping verbal gaps between the two of you to avoid the occurrence of disappointments and feelings of insecurities.

### *Communication reduces the occurrence of infidelity*

Now, let's take a look at communication from a different angle. Ask yourself what communicating with others lead to. When did your spouse fail to share things with you that can be interpreted as not sharing their life with you, right?

Well, it is important to note that when you keep things from your spouse or even avoid a major conversation/argument and desiring to be left alone play a central role in breaking the bond that you share. In other words, when you do this, you are pushing your spouse away.

In as much as this may not be the same case for all couples, lacking an emotional connection with your spouse may arouse the desire to make a connection with someone else. Trust me, you may not want to go down this path, but when your heart is not fulfilled with all of its needs and desires, it will strive to bring itself that satisfaction it wants.

### *Good communication demonstrate respect for your spouse through honesty*

Have you ever found yourself in a situation where you do not wish to talk to your spouse, or your spouse does not want to talk to you and hence end the conversation right there and then?

Well, the truth is that this may work for you at least once or twice. However, over time, you may need to add in a few lies just so that you can get out of the situation. Note that, at this point, it is no longer avoidance; it is now backed up with a pack of lies!

Now, the most important thing you need to note is, when there is nothing to hide from your significant other, there is no need to introduce false information. What this does is that it destroys the chances of you having a beautiful life you have always wanted with your spouse.

At first, it may start as an innocent thing to keep stuff from your spouse. However, with time, it is this kind of behavior that highlights your lack of respect for them. It is high time that you become honest with them at least that is what you owe them. They need to know what is going on in your life, mind, and heart so that you can both handle the situation and get ahead with life.

That said, you have to bear in mind that communication in marriage or any other relationship for that matter is a two-way street without any red lights. When you are communicating with your spouse, it is much more than just sharing what you both have in mind. You cannot drop your frustrations, anger, and news at your spouse and then walk away like nothing just happened.

Understand that communicating simply means that you have to be present for each other. You have to be there when your spouse needs you to comfort them both physically and emotionally. Get over the belief that as a couple, you just say what you feel and walk out of the room.

Opening yourself to your spouse means that you welcome the possibility of receiving information from them as well. In life, whether marriage or elsewhere, we all desire to be needed and wanted by someone. When you are there for each other in marriage, you will be able to face problems and issues together. Nothing will be tough for you. There will be no argument big enough to threaten to break your relationship.

Indeed, communication is a process, but the most important thing is to learn that process so that it can bring you and your spouse closer. When you both learn how to communicate with each other, you develop a unique language. This is not to say that the process of learning effective communication is easy!

Trust me; it is hardly a natural skill. According to research, it is the quality and quantity of communication that plays a key role in bringing couples closer and improving marriages. Therefore, it is your responsibility as a couple to conduct experiments with various communication approaches and ensure that you make the process both fun and productive.

### *Importance of counseling before marriage*

If you are not yet married and are reading this book, bravo! This is a great step when preparing to get married. One thing that you have to understand is that marriage is an exciting engagement that is often followed by a range of plans and activities for the wedding.

At this point, much of the details of your communication may take a focus on the wedding. If you are not careful, the wedding may take the place of even much more important discussions about your future as a married couple. When you seek marriage counseling ahead of your marriage, you are simply increasing your chances of enjoying a satisfying union together. Yes, you may have fallen in love with each other, but you have to understand that a happily ever after takes lots of effort and preparation!

### *Marriage triangle*

There are three major factors that constitute a marriage triangle. These factors include; couple traits, individual traits, and context of the relationship.

Based on a study conducted by Jeffrey H. Larsen on marriage preparation, such individual traits as self-esteem, beliefs, and interpersonal skills affect how one approached marriage. Understand that expectations are not everything! However, they affect everything.

One thing that you need to bear in mind is that marriage counseling brings into focus expectations. It is about bringing them on the table for discussions to ensure that problems are kept at bay.

Some of the couple's traits that play an important role in marriage include their goals, values, communication as well as conflict resolution skills. It is with the help of a marriage counselor that a couple can build on their strength and come up with various ways of overcoming their weaknesses. Realize that your contexts and that of your relationship constitute some of the baggage you bring with you from your past. One of the best ways you can deal with these issues is having an objective third party before crossing the threshold.

### *Married individuals*

There are three major entities to a healthy marriage; two individuals/partners and the marriage itself. If your marriage is going to be successful, then you have to pay attention to each other's identities and your identity as a couple.

Here, you have to be careful about the degree of individuation. In other words, what is your ability to maintain your identity within the context of your marriage? This degree of individuation will often depend on your traits as well as past experiences.

When you seek marriage counseling before becoming united in marriage as a couple, you will be in a better position to learn your strengths and weaknesses. This goes a long way in ensuring that you learn various suggestions and approaches that will help increase your awareness for the sake of your relationship with your significant other.

### Commitment

One of the primary benefits of seeking marriage counseling is showing how committed you are to the success of your marriage. It is through premarital counseling that a couple is offered an opportunity to plan how they will journey through marriage together as an entity. Most importantly, counseling before marriage offers you and your spouse-to-be an opportunity to develop critical problem-solving strategies together.

Realize that when you come into a marriage with

the expectation that every plan will fall in place is only a recipe for disaster. There is a difference between walking blindly and expecting the best but also knowing how to handle situations when the worst happens. It is critical always to have a backup plan in case you both fall into moments of crises so that you can handle issues with so much hope and humor. This way, you protect your marriage from stress and dissatisfaction.

## *Enrichment*

The other benefit of always seeking counseling before committing to the institution of marriage is that it offers you a guide to having your lives enriched as an entity. Growing up in your own individual families will not teach you everything there is to know about marriage. Going to school will also not guarantee that you learn everything about marriage. However, when you go through counseling before marriage, you gather information and techniques that will help you to go through marriage fully aware of ways to enhance being a couple from just gazing into each other's eyes to learning the love language together.

Indeed, marriage is a learning curve that ultimately brings mutual benefits to your relationship so that you are better prepared to be happy in each other's life. In other words, when you choose to walk every step together and learn everything there is to learn about marriage together with so much humility and commitment, then your marriage will enjoy a great deal of satisfaction.

# Chapter 3
# Common marriage communication mistakes

One thing that you will note is that a simple bad habit is what gets couples into trouble. Once your marriage is on a rough patch, it gives room for negativity to grow. This is when issues begin to escalate because both spouses repeat their mistakes over and over again. But the most crucial question here is, "what are these common communication mistakes we should look out for, and how do we fix them?"

### *Mistake 1 Yelling at your spouse*

It is common that when we are angry, we tend to raise our voice mainly because anger stirs up so much tension. As that tension begins to build up, the body looks for ways to try and release or express that anger. One of the fastest ways to expel that is by yelling at your spouse.

What many people fail to realize is that by yelling at their spouse, they are simply causing more trouble than relief. When you unleash that tension, it may feel good at first. However, notice that the sense of satisfaction you draw from this act is only short-lived. There is a high likelihood that everything and anything you say when you are burning with anger will only add more fuel to the fire.

It is essential to understand that yelling often tends to unleash a lot of strong and negative emotional feelings. It does not matter what you are trying to communicate because what will take center stage is the emotional feelings you have. It is this very emotion that will capture the attention to the listener.

What is even more unfortunate is the fact that the message you are trying to communicating at that point becomes diminished or even worse misunderstood. This is mainly the case because what you are doing is setting up your partner to be defensive and frustrated instead if supporting them to be understanding and responsive.

You need to realize that you can express strong emotions when you speak. The truth is, you are not a robot! By yelling at your spouse, you are crossing the lines and are setting the stage for a heated emotional argument that can be communicated if you both calm down and talk.

Yes, your emotional feelings maybe the message

you are trying to put across. However, what you need to realize is that having a purely emotional exchange is only a recipe for an exhaustive and destructive habit. At some level, you will need to communicate in a manner that permits you to simply move past your emotions rather than trying to fuel them.

*Let your words speak volumes to your spouse*

One important point to note is that when you keep your emotional feelings in check, the message that you are trying to communicate to your spouse will shine through. Well, by no means does this mean that you should try to shove out your emotions. The truth is, in some instances, your emotions are a very pertinent component of the whole situation.

However, what you need to remember is that the essence of communicating is so that the other party can clearly understand where you are coming from. To achieve that, the channels through which you communicate has to favor both the sender and the receiver. When you indulge in excessive emotions, you are simply allowing all that to interfere with communication. Therefore, take time to ride off the wave of emotional feelings so that you can settle and be sober enough to listen and communicate effectively.

The other option you need to consider is taking a quick exercise before you pick the conversation from where you left it. Working out is one of the best ways to lower your stress levels. Additionally, it has been shown that physical exercises can distract one from their intense emotional feelings.

Trust me; it is pretty difficult to focus on your emotional feelings and troubles, especially when you can hardly breathe. It may be helpful at this point to distract your mind from everything that is going on around you. Take time to write down what you would like to say so that you ensure that you deliver your intended message the best and clear way possible.

Don't shy off from talking about the things that make you feel very emotional. The best thing you need to realize is that by keeping your spouse by your side during this time, you can overcome the problems you are facing. Instead of pushing them away and creating more and more problems.

## Mistake 2 Having a competitive attitude

Look around you, can you see competition going on? I guess your response is Yes! Well, the truth is that competition is all around us. You are probably watching a football game, getting ahead at your workplace, preparing for a job interview, or even preparing some Christmas displays in the neighborhood among others. All these are forms of competitions that someone will always be striving hard to win. There are certain areas of your life where you are probably trying to get ahead, and your marriage may be one of them. The thing that you need to realize here is that when one of you is a winner, then both spouses are considered losers.

The little cooking competition in the neighborhood may be ok, and you probably will rib each other out with all the cookout winning predictions. But the truth is that that is just about it! You have to understand that anything that is not mutual and playful has the possibility of creating walls between the two parties.

In some instances, you will find yourself creating a case at the back of your mind, and then creating a very long list of bullet points for the disagreement you envision with your spouse. The truth is that you may win all these arguments. However, what you do not realize is that you are exhausting and demoralizing your spouse more than anything else in the world.

*Think about the reason why you feel the need to win*

If you are someone with emotional insecurities, the chances are that you will try to overcompensate by trying hard to look superior to your spouse. This is mainly because when you stay at the top, you feel that you are much stronger and more confident than the other. Research shows that you will likely have trouble when you are vulnerable because you feel as though your insecurities are being exposed and would possibly clash with your beliefs of being successful.

Does this sound like you? If yes, the most important question to ask is whether your spouse gets tired of your victory dance and your desire to always have the upper hand. It is time for you to come back down to earth a little. The chances are that your spouse is happier seeing you with some imperfections. Yes, you may not be used to seeing your spouse show so much tenderness towards you.

However, the bottom line is that if you married a great person, then there is nothing you stand to lose. Instead, you have so much more to gain from your marriage. Therefore, quit the competitive attitude and the desire always to win arguments and consider how much satisfaction comes from compromising to make your partner feel safe and strengthen the relationship.

### *Mistake 3 Making marriage about me instead of we*

Is there are chatter going on in your mind? Ever stopped to listen to what it has to say? In most cases, it focuses on you. It is interested in what you like, how you messed things up, what it is that you have coming up on your schedule, what your expectations are, and so on.

Naturally, there is so much bias in this chatter because it is mainly from your perception of things and how you perceive the situation. But one thing that you need to ask yourself is what does a chatter about your spouse say? Is it about how much fun you are going to have later, and what you expect from them, what mood you are in and so on?

Most of the time, when we allow our selfish desires to get ahead of what our relationships and marriage needs, then we lose the point. You must start shaking off that self-centered view so that you can see the bigger picture.

*Consider your spouse's point of view and purpose to make their day better*

If you are looking to nurture a great marriage, then you have to be willing to show your spouse generosity and considerate behavior. Rather than trying to crack your head figuring out whether they will load the dishwasher right, focus on doing something that your spouse will appreciates. Try to put a smile of their face.

Well, the truth is that they may not throw you a ticker-tape parade for it, but the most important thing is that you do not allow yourself to get caught up in the thought of "what is in it for me?" ever again.

When you remain thoughtful and generous towards your spouse, the truth is that it will spark something within them that will, in most cases, be a positive response. In other words, if they were going to say something, they may choose to hold back their comments to see whether your new trend is going to stick. They are likely looking to see whether this response is just a gimmick act or it is indeed a positive habit you are cultivating.

Once they see that your efforts are genuine and consistent, the message will be clear. Therefore, you must allow those selfish thoughts and acts towards your spouse to pass so that you can keep showing them how much you love them.

The other secret that you need to note is that

feelings often follow actions. What this means is that you may not feel loved at first when you start show generosity in your actions. Well, if they do not say anything at first, you do not have to beat yourself up for it. Keep showing love and generosity. The more you do this, the more this comes naturally to you and hence more love towards your significant other.

### Mistake #4 Splitting housework evenly

You may already be asking yourself what could be wrong with splitting house chores 50/50 between you and your spouse. Well, one thing that you need to understand is that when you do this, you are opening yourselves to keeping scores.

What happens when you feel that your spouse is not taking a fair share? The truth is, there are times when you will feel that you are taking up lots of the work at home while your spouse gets to relax and watch a movie! Trust me, when you start feeling like there is unfairness in how work has been shared between the two of you, you open the door for anger and resentment.

*Openly discuss who does what*

You both must talk about who does what openly.

Who is going to cook, clean, maintain the house, cars, and care for the children, among other important activities in your household? The thing is, when you feel that work is divided mutually based on an agreed-upon approach, each one of you feels that their contribution is highly valued.

What you will notice is that so many couples often split housework based on what they are best at. There is one that handles grocery shopping, bills, and laundry better than the other. There may be one that does yard work and car maintenance even better. The truth is, there are times when you will end up doing more while the other does less, and vice versa. However, the key here is that you should not keep track. Otherwise, you will begin to see things that do not exist!

### *Mistake #5 Setting unrealistic expectations for your marriage*

According to research, most therapists have revealed that what kills most marriages is often failure for one to accept what they are, their spouse, and marriage what they are. You met your spouse, dated, fell in love, and got married, right? But the problem comes in when we think that the only thing that keeps marriage standing is love and respect. But really, it is communication and acceptance that does. It is the glue that keeps your marriage together!

Marriages are not perfect. They are very far from anything perfect. Some storms will threaten to tear your marriage apart if you let them. However, when you communicate effectively with your spouse and accept your union as it is, you will accept that it is not always wine and roses. You will be able to weather the storms together, and that is what will strengthen your union and keep you going for as long as you both live.

### *Mistake #6 Thinking that sexual issues do not matter*

It is important to note that sex is a very important component of any many marriages. This means that you both have to be on the same page as far as your sexual intimacy is concerned. If you have issues in your sex life, then you have a very big problem.

However, understand that most of the sexual issues couples go through are treatable, but you both have to be willing to seek medical or mental health help from professionals. When you take the time to identify what the problem is, you will also be able to fix these difficulties, hence making sex better. Fixing sexual intimacy issues can fix other problems in the marriage as well. The main reason for this is that it is truly hard to be distant from someone you are connected to.

When you lack a good sex life, then you both are missing the intimacy that can only be found from quality marital sex. Bear in mind that, checking in with the doctor when one of you has low libido or the sexual intercourse hurts is an important step towards healing. But you are not going to cross the bridge if both of you are not willing to communicate with one another.

There could be some underlying issues that both of you need to address. However, even if health is not the issue here, talking through your difficulties and struggles with a therapist will go a long way in opening up your communication to a rather tricky situation and topic.

### *Mistake #7 Anger Issues*

In a relationship, one thing that you need to be careful about is your anger and how to keep it in check. One thing that you need to realize is that when you allow anger to get the best of you, then the chances are that you are going to hurt your relationship so badly.

When one of you is not able to deal with anger issues effectively, it opens the door for so much damage. Therefore, you both must learn how to successfully deal with anger so that you eliminate the possibility of it building up and becoming a weapon that can hurt your marriage. Talk to your therapist about it for you to identify the root cause of your anger and nib it at the bud before it grows out of hand.

Ever heard of the saying "never go to bed angry?" Well, this is something that most couples often misinterpret. They end up staying up all night trying to resolve an argument they had. The truth is, this is not the best way to go! It is one approach that adds more salt to injury.

Rather than beating yourself up all night over a disagreement you had with your spouse, try to go to sleep and get a better perspective of the whole situation. When you sleep on it, you allow that anger to subside, something that will give you clarity on how to handle the situation in a sober way. If you try to resolve the issue into the wee hours of the night, you only risk getting exhausted and giving room for more resentment.

So, yes, it is alright to go to bed angry sometimes. Allow your mind and body to get enough rest. Sleep on the issue, and when the morning comes, you can reconvene the resolution process when both of you are well-rested, have an open mind, and are less riled up.

## Mistake #8 Expecting that your spouse will read your mind

There are times when we have all made the mistake of thinking that our spouse knows what we need, even without telling them. We assume that because you are both married, they can read your mind and know what you are thinking. You think that because you had a rough day at work, they can tell that and hug us. We think that he will wash the car because it is very dirty and going to use it the next day.

Well, one thing that you have to note is that this is close to impossible. What you are doing is just allowing yourself to be resentful if your spouse fails to do what you expected them to "in your head."

*The best thing that you can do is to be transparent with them.*

Simply give your spouse all the information they need. Do not expect them to know things they cannot know if you have not told them. Simply tell them that you have had a rough day and would not want to be bothered. Tell them to remember to wash the car on their way home because you will be using it the following day.

Just tell them what they need to know! Remember that communication is the key to ensuring that your marriage is functional, happy, and brings all the joy that you have always prayed for. It just has to start with you!

### *Mistake #9 Parenting differences*

We all have our philosophies about parenting. There is something that you believe in as far as parenting and will always want to adhere to that line of thought no matter what, right? The truth is, so many parenting disagreements arise from the fact that both parents have varying points of view on what the right parenting should or should not be like.

For instance, you may prefer to allow your kids to make mistakes and then face the consequences naturally while your spouse prefers a more proactive way of preventing children from making mistakes in the first place. This kind of difference is what brings about conflict in marriages.

It is important to note that when your parenting

style is different from that employed by your spouse, it can get to you and at its worst, bring about destruction. If you are not careful, this may drive a wedge between you and your spouse creating distance between you and among your children.

Understand that parenting is part of the marriage package. Each one of you came from different backgrounds and parenting systems, and look you both loved each other and are married. If you are going to raise your children in a happy marriage, then you both have to constantly assess your parenting and adjust based on each one of your children's development and temperaments.

Additionally, you have to be willing to do parenting together with your spouse as a unit. The only way to do this is to be willing to compromise where necessary. It is also important that the strategy you choose to employ while parenting is informed by what is in the best interest of your child at the very top of the list. Ask yourselves what your goals for raising your children are and how each one of them comes into fulfilling these goals.

## *Mistake #10 Financial disagreements*

It does not matter how much money a couple makes because when there are financial disagreements, the marriage is on fire! Financial problems can lead to a huge conflict irrespective of whether a couple is in debt, has no budget, cannot agree in their expenditure, among other issues.

One thing that you have to understand is that when you got married, each one of you came into the marriage institution with their attitudes about money. If there is no clarity on such things as how much money is to be saved, spent, earned, and used, then you are headed for so much trouble. The thing is, when financial issues are not discussed, they can grow bigger than life itself and tear you apart no matter how devoted you are to each other.

To avoid such conflicts from taking a toll on your marriage, you mustn't keep the money a mystery in your marriage. You have to start by creating a realistic budget, come up with joint short- and long-term money goals that you stick to set some funds aside for emergencies and work on reviewing your financial goals together annually. This way, you ensure that there is transparency in your finances and that each one of you is comfortable and knows where you stand as far as money is concerned.

### *Mistake #11 Underestimating small changes*

Have you been through a change in marriage before? How did that affect your marriage?

The truth is, when you get married, there are so many changes that will happen. Interestingly, couples are often tempted to look at the changes and blame their spouses for the outcome. In other words, small changes can be the reason why there are resentment and bitterness in your relationship.

There are times when you will hear a spouse asking their partner to quit their job to take care of the growing house chore demands or childcare, among others. Yes, so many chores at home can be overwhelming when both of you are working. The secret is for you to consider smaller changes that you both can compromise to help better the situation.

Think of cooking your meals over the weekend, or hiring occasional cleaning services so that none of you will have to quit their job to do these things. Rather than going for one grand change that might hurt the other, simply look for incremental changes that will aim at improving your situation.

That said, it is important to understand the importance of communication in marriage. It is the key to having a good marriage. Understand that listening is the most important component of communication. When your partner does not feel that you hear them, this can make it impossible to achieve success within your marriage.

When your spouse knows that you care enough to pay attention to what they have to say, it can go a very long way in keeping your marriage together even if the issue is not immediately resolved.

Ask yourself whether your marriage could use some direct communication between you and your spouse. You both have to be willing to honesty discuss your feelings so that each one of you knows what the other needs from them. However, such feelings as fear, hopelessness, and pride threaten to get in the way of direct communication.

When you fail to communicate with your spouse directly, you end up suffering in silence or even worse, take a passive route to communication. One thing that you have to remember is that you hold the key to a healthy marriage. You can only get things right by offering your spouse a word of encouragement instead of always criticizing them.

With positive communication comes basic habits such as expressing intentional gentleness, paying attention intently to what your spouse is saying, and then validating them. When you have these habits, you can drive change and growth into your marriage.

# Chapter 4
# How to Fix communication issues in marriage

There are so many ways in which one can fix problems in their marriage. Well, let me start by saying that my partner and I were blissfully in love and thrilled when we first got married and were going for our honeymoon.

Then, came the fifth day when we had our very first argument. The truth is, this put us on a very slippery slope moving fast into desperation. Trust me, within the very first year of marriage, my partner and I were convinced that we were not meant for one another. We felt as though we were both condemned to a loveless marriage.

Want to know what the tangible problem was? – Poor communication. I would come home and meet him watching football and when I asked anything he would be like "I can't believe you have not made dinner yet, am hungry" He would go on "Plus, what time are coming home? Where have you been all this time? You better get dinner ready coz am starving!"

I am not saying that my husband was the only one with all the arguments. Well, I had my fair share too. We both could express anything we wanted, and this resorted to us hurting each other with words. Instead of building each other up, we chose to tear each other apart. This caused us deep emotional pain.

We had endured so much hurt and pain that we lost hope in ever communicating effectively in our marriage. The despair was so overwhelming. However, we did not just throw away our marriage; we signed up for counseling and started learning the importance of intentional communication.

At first, I thought that was the *most damn* thing I have ever heard! I thought to myself that intentional communication was way too simple for us to be spending money going to therapy. With time, I saw how things slowly started improving, and I got off my high horse. I thought to myself that if indeed communication was simple, everyone could be doing it right. Everything we do and how we do it would give glory to God, and we would reflect His image as Ephesians 4:29 tells us.

The truth is, giving glory to God did not define how I chose to communicate with my partner. In some ways, you may be like me at the time. You could be struggling to communicate well with your spouse, parents, children, or fiancé. One thing that you have to understand is that there is nothing permanent in this world. We did not get stuck in a loveless marriage. We chose to change our story. We chose to work on our issues and learn about communication in marriage; however tough that was.

Here are some of the things we did to fix our issues;

### *Follow the principle of first response*

This states that the course of any conflict is not determined by who initiates it but by the person that responds to it. When you feel that your spouse is picking a fight with you, it is easy to start feeling that it's okay to strike back at them with words. You think to yourself that he/she has been doing this over and over and you are sick and tired of it. You want to put him/her in their rightful place.

Yes, you may feel that you are correct to do so. However, one thing that you need to understand is that your partner does not have the power to decide whether to start a fight. The power rests on the person that responds. According to

Proverbs 15:1, the scripture tells us that a gentle response turns away wrath while a harsh word stirs up strife.

Look at the example of Jesus Christ; he had the track record with this principle. There were so many instances when the Pharisees and Scribes came to question His way of doing things. They initiated almost every communication because their major intention was to defraud Jesus and push Him to His limits.

But how many cases were they successful? None!

The main reason why they failed was that the power to decide the direction the argument or conflict takes rested upon Jesus, who in this case was the responder (Luke 20:19-26). Am not saying that your spouse is a Pharisee or Scribe. However, communication in marriage takes this form as well. When you choose to follow in the steps of Jesus Christ, your life and marriage will turn around for the best. Your spouse's tantrums do not give you a license to throw tantrums as well. By following this principle, you are being called to take a negative comment and redirect it towards the positive side for the greater good.

### *Follow the principle of a physical touch*

Have you ever thought about how difficult it is to be mad at someone while touching them so lovingly and tenderly?

You may be thinking, but what is the best time to apply this principle? Well, the truth is, you had better apply this principle after an argument starts. That said, the best time is when you know that you are going to have a difficult conversation with your spouse about something that might stir up tension between the two of you.

Well, you know what these difficult conversations are in your marriage. It could be discussions about your children, in-laws, finances, or investment options, among others. For us, what often took us to sit down and have a talk was always about our communication. Trust me; those were tough discussions!

We would sit down, pray together, and touch. In most cases, my partner and I would sit on opposite ends of the dining table with my husband's legs stretched out across mine while we held hands across the table. There are so many ways in which you can apply the principle of touch. As you talk to each other, there are things that you can inevitably notice about your partner.

Yes, this is a serious discussion, and there are times when the conversation drifts towards conflict, and you stop touching each other. Certainly, you will find the same thing I found- it is difficult to fight when you are touching your spouse tenderly and with love. Gaze into his/her eyes. You have a choice to make; stop fighting so that you can keep touching, or stop touching and keep fighting! Which one shall it be?

Understand that this kind of touching has played a key role in helping us communicate better with each other and lovingly resolve our issues. Well, most of our conflicts have even ended up in some steamy lovemaking! Am just saying that it does not have to tear you apart. It can draw you closer to each other more than ever. It opens your eyes to the kind of person you fell in love with and causes you to fall in love all over again.

This principle is deterrent from arguing. When you find yourselves drifting into an argument, this should be your physical and visual cue that your conversation is no longer bringing glory to God as it should. When you notice it, then you know that you have to correct it so that you can both get back on the right track.

God designed the institution of marriage not to be broken whatsoever until death does you part. So whatever issues you face, you have to work them out together so that you enjoy all the promises he spoke over the institution of marriage.

### *Apply the principle of proper timing*

Here, the principle is that the success of any conversation can be multiplied only if the timing is carefully selected. According to Proverbs 15:23, the scripture tells that the man finds joy in responding promptly and that a timely word is truly good.

Typically, for my husband and I, our conversations were always made at dinner time. This is the time when we both have come home from work and are catching up on the days' events. We have been blessed with five children, and as you can imagine, our dinner table is active and quite busy. This means that there is no way we are going to have a prolonged and meaningful discussion practically.

In other words, if there is anything that has happened that needs us to discuss, we would wait for the children to go to bed before we have started ironing out our issues. When you choose to bring up a difficult conversation during dinner, what you are typically doing is inviting frustrations and ineffective communication.

Let us consider our marriage scenario. I am someone my husband likes to describe as an intentional homemaker with brilliant ideas on how to improve and serve our family better. When I am contemplating a new approach to family weekends, I take weeks thinking about it, planning it out in my head until I feel that it is fully baked and ready to share. This is awesome. Well, probably not worth sharing on a Sunday afternoon when my husband and our sons are watching football!

One problem I have is that of poor timing. For instance, we have been downstairs enjoying our normal conversation, and when it's time to go to bed and the lights are off, I start asking my husband serious questions I would have hours earlier. Bedtime is not the best time to have extensive discussions.

Well, there are times when discussions are critical to have at that time. It is during those times when the football game is switched off, and we can have a talk or the lights go back on, and we can talk for hours. However, this is not a rule; instead, they are referred to as exceptions.

Therefore, ensure that the majority of the time, you are more strategic in your timings for serious conversations in marriage.

### *Follow the principle of mirroring*

This requires that your understanding of others can be increased if we constantly measure it during conversations. In Proverbs 22:17, the scripture tells us that we should incline our ears towards hearing wise words and then applying our minds to knowledge.

There are times when you say something and meant what you said, but then the person you are telling it hears something completely different. How did you feel? Frustrating, right? In the same way in marriage, there are times when you say one thing and your spouse hears something else.

If you are not certain, your spouse is getting what you are saying; you must check with them to know whether they ask what you meant by what you said. You can even take it a notch higher to find out from them whether they understood what you are saying.

This is what I refer to as mirroring. It plays a significant role in testing whether they heard you properly. The same way, you can misunderstand what your spouse is saying. To avoid this from happening, repeat what they said back to them. You can say something like, "So, what you are saying is..." Then you can also use your words to tell your spouse what you understood they said.

Once you have done this, the next phase is the most important part of mirroring. This is the point where you allow your spouse to give you an affirmation over what they said or correct what you just interpreted from their words.

In our marriage, as we learned this principle, I realized that there are so many times when we hear what we want to hear, and that is not what the other person was saying. It would make me mad when my husband had a negative summaries of my statements. I realized that these were things that stirred up more conflict in the first place.

The secret is not for you to defend yourself. You must allow your spouse the freedom to speak their mind, heart, and soul. Give them time to express what they have in mind with utmost honesty. What is interesting is that when you start mirroring each other's conversations, you learn that your summaries become accurate. In the same way, your reactions may be negative because you do not know how they expose you to your spouse. Give them the chance to clarify what you are saying so that as the conversation grows, you are both on the same page.

The point of mirroring conversations is not so that you can be right. It is not about defending yourself. However, it is about helping you, and your spouse knows whether what you are hearing them/you say is accurate. When you seek to understand each other's statements instead of making yourself be understood, you are priming yourself for success with this principle.

### *Exercise the principle of prayer*

Here, one thing that you need to understand is that successful communication is more likely achieved when we allow God to be an active participant and guide from the very beginning.

This is the most straightforward principle I have ever used! While that has been evident in our marriage, you have to realize that it requires your close attention. Most of us have become so used to hearing the prayer that the importance of it pass us by.

It does not matter what principle you are used to when communicating with your spouse in marriage. It doesn't even matter what subject you are both talking about or the scenario that underlies your prayers. There are many times when people overestimate their abilities to effectively and righteously communicate with their partners. This is something that we observed during our first year of marriage.

Bear in mind that there are times when you will eventually and inevitably sin in your communication with your spouse. When you begin to drift apart, you will drift away from God and the purpose he intended for you and your marriage. The truth is that the choice lies with you. Are you going to allow pride to puff you up, or are you going to demonstrate humility by stopping right where you are and then asking God to help redeem your communication?

Am not saying that I wasted our first year of marriage, but all I can say is that I wish someone had told me Evangelist R.A. Torrey's words;

*"The reason why many fail in battle is that they wait until the hour of battle. The reason why others succeed is that they had gained their victory on their knees long before the battle came ... Anticipate your battles; fight them on*

*your knees before temptation comes, and you will always have victory."*

Today, couples go through so many difficulties because of awkwardness. It is because they have not cultivated the culture of praying together. This means that as they begin to like less and less of each other amid unconstructive conversations, the thought of praying together as a family appears less and less appealing.

The easiest fix that my husband and I learned was to start praying together both in the good and the bad times. You can start with a minute of prayer right before you both retire to bed. Do this regularly as a family before meals. You can even go a notch higher to pick one day in the week when you dedicate your children to God in prayer. Another day you can do prayers over your marriage, among other things.

The truth is that one of the enormous benefits you will see in your family is that the regularity of prayer will make communication breakdowns in your marriage less probable. It will make praying amid communication issues highly likely. That is the beauty of making God the center of your marriage.

With these principles, you have to understand

that transformation will never end. It is not like you to become an angel and never make mistakes. The truth is that there will be times when you mess up, but the good thing is that God will keep working in, on and through you.

Remember, when we started this section, I said that we were convinced that we were not meant for each other. We believed that my husband and I were condemned to a loveless marriage. Today, we cannot imagine knowing, loving, doing, and enjoying anyone else other than each other.

Yes, the relationship you and your spouse have is different from mine. But the truth is that your spouse should always be the one person you cannot be without as long as you both are alive. Whether you like it or not, communication in marriage is the one tool God gave us to knit our minds, hearts, and actions. If you are willing to apply these principles into your marriage situation, then you are just one step away from success. You and I have been called to have a God-honoring communication. Therefore, take a step forward in faith and humility and let God transform your marriage so that you can live the life He designed for you and your spouse.

# Chapter 5
# Communicating when angry

One of the things that makes communication difficult is when you allow your anger to get in the way of your conversations. You must eliminate your anger issues first so that when you have a conversation, you create and maintain a healthy relationship.

To reiterate what I already mentioned previous, your spouse is not a mind reader. They do not know what you need unless you tell them. But the question is, how do you tell them what you need? Do you say it with anger? Well, if you do, then chances are that their response will determine the direction of the whole conversation. It gets worse if they respond defensively or angrily.

An important point to note is that communicating without anger takes a lot of self-awareness most people lack. The most common mistake people make is exploding and saying hurtful words they will wish they could take back. Even though your spouse did something that was entirely out of line, choosing to communicate without anger goes a long way in getting things cleared up fast so that you avoid resentment.

Let's face it; being in an intimate relationship, much less a marriage is not something easy. Ensuring that you and your spouse have everything you need takes a lot of openness, honesty, and zero blame games. You are both humans who are far from perfect! You cannot always put your partner first if you are bogged down by life's circumstances that you allow to spin out of control. The same thing goes for your partner.

Now, let us consider a situation where you are upset about your spouse's behavior. What do you do? You start overthinking and ruminating over the whole situation. You allow the tape of your conversation to play in your mind over and over again. You keep revisiting who did what and who said what.

Before long, you curve your spouse into a monster, something that he is not. You fell in love with him, and the chances are that he is nothing like a monster; otherwise, why would you be with him in the first place?

One thing that you need to realize is that your

spouse is probably trying hard to meet his obligations so that you both can be happy together. In the meantime, you feel as though you have been put on the back burner, ignored and mistreated. Yes, this feeling is not good, but the question is, are you familiar with the whole situation?

When something similar takes place, communicating with anger, and yelling at your spouse is likely to happen. You probably will start saying hurtful things that you cannot take back. What you are merely doing is making the whole situation worse than it already is. You will push him away and what happens is that he will wall off and will not feel heard at all.

One thing that I have noticed when this happens is that you start convincing yourself that it is not so big of a deal. However, the truth is that you cannot let it go, and it starts eating into your relationship bits by bits until what is left of it is resentment and unprocessed issues.

But what if you choose to be clear, centered, and emotionally aware of what is going on? Well, the truth is that you will be better placed to handle the whole situation with an open heart, faith, and so much grace.

You first need to discover what your core needs are when you are upset. Realize that your emotions at that point are like waves; they come and go away. However, beneath these waves of emotions are important information. The question is, where do they end up?

Well, one thing that is important to note is that if you fail to process these emotions or even at least recognize that they exist, you will be repressing them. Each time you fight with your spouse, you bottle it in and sooner than you think, it all explodes.

You cannot be walking around with that much body weight. This is too much emotional weight that you need to let go. Well, am not going to tell you how to lighten that load, but I will certainly help you stay on the clear from what is upsetting you. This way, you can effectively communicate with your spouse and the people in your life without anger, giving you a better chance of ensuring that all of your needs in marriage are met.

You cannot change your spouse's frustrating behavior. However, what you can do is let him know in a more centered way how his/her behavior affects you. No one likes hurting their loved ones intentionally, at least that is how I

MARRIAGE ADVICE SELF-HELP BOOKS

like to see it. Most of the mistakes we make are unconscious and do not have ill intentions.

Therefore, it is up to you to ensure that you let your spouse know what you need and want from them. Throwing tantrums, pretending to be okay when you are not, and shutting down your emotions is not going to solve anything. It will only poison your marriage more and more each day.

To keep that connection between you and your spouse, you have to learn how to communicate with them without anger effectively. To accomplish, you have first to determine what your core needs are when trapped in an upsetting situation. Once you have that figured out, then it is time that you have to learn how to give that need a clear and a heart-centered voice.

*How do you do that?*

Well, what you need to do is process these emotions before you start communicating with your partner so that you know what your core needs are. Rather than exploding in fit anger when talking to your spouse, these steps are going to help you put things under control. You will not have to avoid the whole situation or suck up.

78

Yes, your anger is valid, but you have to take care of yourself emotionally. This is not your spouse's job.

## Step 1 Notice

The very first step that you need to take is to notice the behavior you have when you are angry. Ask yourself whether your behavior is sabotaging. Are there things that you do when you are angry that you blame yourself later for? Do you feel ashamed of yourself and your actions when angry? Do you curse people, throw utensils on the wall, or even turntables upside down?

One thing that you need to understand is that when you are self-aware of how you cope with anger; your behavior will change for the better.

## Step 2 Name

Once you notice your behavior when feeling angry, then the next thing you need to do is to name these feelings. Let's take a step back for a minute, do you know that anger is an emotional feeling? Realize that anger is the reason why other vulnerable feelings you have are guarded such as sadness and fear, among others.

79

Realize that anger is the thing that is walling you off from having and expressing more vulnerable feelings. When you know what other feelings you have, you stand a better chance of overcoming anger. You must process it.

That said, you and your spouse have to be willing to name the feelings you have and the parts of your body where you feel them. Is it a heaviness in your heart? Is there aching in your stomach? Is it a knot in your throat? What is it; sadness, fear, or anger? Is it a combination of all of them?

Close your eyes and notice whether what you are feeling has a color, shape, or texture. This is what we refer to as emotional energy in the body. This is what seeks your attention. It is screaming from deep within you like a baby. Name it!

### Step 3 Nurture

Now that you have noticed what emotional feelings you have and have even named them and their features, the next thing is for you to nurture that screaming baby. Start by placing your hands on your heart or the belly and whatever parts of your body; you are feeling the emotion. Try as much as you can to hold that energy like a baby.

Understand that it was not your intention to feel this way. That feeling wants your love. Realize that it carries wisdom for you. Ensure that you stay present with that energy. Take in deep and slow breaths while offering it the light of your consciousness. This way, you will begin to feel calm in your mind, body, and soul as it helps you gain access to the wisdom it has to offer you.

### *Step 4 Need*

Once you have had some time to be present and actively feel these emotional energies, the next thing is for you to ask yourself what you need from them. Do not take this question lightly. Remember, it is a pain of your body that will help you overcome anger once and for all. What you are asking yourself is important in helping you figure out what your core needs are and not the need for someone else to change.

Some of these core needs may include; quality time, matter, consistency, consideration, and acknowledgment, among others. Bear in mind that these core needs you are trying to identify are all about you and not your spouse. Once you know what you need, you will notice the body starting to calm down and remain centered.

The trick is for you to focus on your needs. Focus on why you matter rather than staying angry on your partner. Instead of being angry at your spouse, focus closely on what you can do during your quality time. Why do you think that you need consistency and consideration? Find things that you acknowledge about you rather than screaming at your spouse for their acknowledgment.

### *Strategies that will help keep your anger at bay*

There are several strategies you can employ to ensure that you keep your anger at bay for the sake of communicating effectively with your spouse. These strategies include;

### *Relaxation*

There are so many simple relaxation tools that you can employ when angry so that you can calm down. Some of these tools include; relaxing imagery and deep breathing. There are so many books that are created to teach you how to achieve relaxation techniques. The good news is that once you have learned the technique, you can call upon them whenever you are angry.

Start by asking yourself whether you are hot-tempered. Is your partner hot-tempered too? If yes, then you should learn the relaxation technique together.

The first thing you need to do is take a deep breath right from your diaphragm. Do not breathe from your chest as this will not help you calm down. As you breathe in, visualize that breath coming up from your diaphragm.

While doing that, chant these wants; "relax and take it easy." Visualize the relaxation experience. Add in such exercises as yoga to help your muscles feel calm. Keep practicing this each day and use them whenever a tense situation arises so that the body can get used to triggering its use naturally when angry.

*Cognitive restructuring*

You may be wondering what this is. Well, this is referred to as changing your thought process. When you are angry, you will notice that it is so easy to start using curse words, swearing-in colorful terms, and even behaving in a manner that reflects on what your inner thought process is like.

Notice that when you are angry, the mind starts thinking in an overly dramatic way. Instead of allowing this to get the best of you, you need to replace these thoughts with more rational ones.

For example; instead of trying to convince yourself how awful and less talented you are, turn that into a more positive remark like you are awesome and talented. Yes, it may be understandable for you to be upset, but you have to realize that it is not the end of the world. Getting angry will only make the situation worse than it already is.

Be careful not to use such words as "never" when you are referring to yourself and your spouse. The truth is, this kind of system does not work one bit because what you are simply saying is inaccurate. Doing this will only make you justify the whole situation in the first place, and that is no way to get a solution.

Always remind yourself that anger will not solve anything at all. It will not make you feel any better. The truth is that logic beats anger. No matter how much you try to justify anger, it can quickly become irrational. Therefore, you must try using cold hard logic on yourself. Always bear in mind that the world is not out there to get you. Everyone experiences rough patches in life, and you are not an exception. When you do this, you will get a balanced perspective of the whole situation.

If you allow anger to get the best of you, you will start demanding such things as appreciation, fairness, willingness, and agreement, among other things. Yes, everybody desires these things, and when we fail to get them, we end up hurt and disappointed.

As part of cognitive restructuring, angry people tend to have awareness if their demanding nature. They end up translating their expectations into desires. In other words, instead of using such phrases as "I must have this," use the phrase "I would like to have this." This way, when you do not get what you wanted, you do not become hurt, disappointed, and frustrated. Even better, you do not end up angry. Angry people use anger as a way to avoid feeling hurt, but the truth is that that does not work and most certainly will not cause the hurt to go away.

*Problem-solving*

At times, our anger and frustrations may arise because of real problems we cannot run away from in our lives. The truth is, not all anger is misplaced. In fact, in some cases, expressing that anger is a healthy and natural response to difficult situations.

85

Ever heard of the cultural belief that every problem has a solution? Well, the truth is that this is not 100% accurate and is the cause of many frustrations people go through when they cannot find a solution to their problems. The best attitude you can bring to such a situation is not to pay attention to the solution but on the approach on how to handle the problem first hand.

Start by coming up with a plan and then implement it. Then keep checking on the progress every step of the way. Decide to give it your very best without beating yourself up if you do not find an immediate solution to your issue. If you approach every situation with the best intentions, you lower the likelihood of losing patience along the way. You eliminate the all-or-nothing kind of thinking, especially when the problem does not get resolved right away.

*Better communication*

One of the mistakes couples make is jumping into conclusion, which is, in most cases, inaccurate. When you get into a heated discussion with your spouse, the first thing that you have to do is take a step back, slow down and take time to think through the whole situation and your response.

Try to tame your tongue not to say the very first thing that comes into your mind. Always take time to carefully think through every thought that comes to your mind so that what comes through your mouth is upright and not hurtful. The same time, it is important that you pay attention to what your spouse has to say. Then take your time to digest what they said before you can give your response.

Additionally, think through what underlies your anger. If you would like to have some space and freedom while your spouse desires more closeness and connection, tell them what it is that you want. Rather than retaliating by painting them as a warden, jailer or even albatross around your neck, think about what that would make them feel. Be considerate in your response.

Yes, it is natural to get defensive whenever someone criticizes us, but the best thing is to do nothing about it. Pay attention to what underlies your response; neglect, and feelings of being unloved. You may need to exercise patience in your questioning, or taking a breathing space. However, the bottom line should be that you do not allow your anger to spin out of control. When you keep your cool, you are letting the whole situation from getting out of hand and tearing down everything that you both have worked hard to build together as a couple.

*Use humor*

Did you know that some silly humor can help defuse anger in so many ways? Well, one thing that I have learned over the years is that humor goes a long way in helping you keep a more balanced perspective. Do not allow anger to lead you into calling your spouse names or using some imaginative phrase.

Just take a step back to think about what that word would mean. If you call your spouse a "*dirtbag*," picture a bag full of dirt watching a movie with you, cooking and dining with you, or even in bed together doing you know what! Whenever these names come into your mind to ensure that it takes the edge on your fury. Instead, choose to use humor to help in easing the whole situation.

One shocking thing about anger is that it clouds your judgment, making you feel as though you are morally right. It makes you feel as though changing your plans or anything that blocks them has no dignity.

When you feel this way, you must imagine

yourself as a god or goddess that owns the whole universe, making strides alone and having your way in all circumstances as others defer to you. Try to bring in as much imagination to your imaginary scenes as much as you can. The chances are that you will realize that your actions are making you unreasonable. You will learn that the things you are mad at are unimportant and the person you are taking out your anger on is the best gift from God to you.

However, when using humor, remember to take these two cautions; do not try to laugh it off and do not use sarcastic humor. This is because humor is meant to help you be more constructive in what you say. Using harsh sarcasm can stir up more strife and resentment. The good thing is for you to realize that anger is but an emotion that is often accompanied by ideas. If you examine these ideas closely, they will make you laugh!

## Change your environment

One thing that you need to realize is that our immediate environment may be the cause of our irritation and touchy mood. The problems and responsibilities that lay right in front of us may weight us down and make us angry and trapped.

What you need here is to give yourself a break!

Ensure that you schedule some personal time every day when you get away from all the hustles and bustles of the day. A good example here is a working mother with the standing rule that once she gets home from work every evening, the first 15 minutes are just for her and no one should try to talk to her unless the house is on fire! You can also come up with your version of spending some "me time" so that you not only feel better placed to handle the demands that await you but also ensures that you do not blow it up with your spouse.

# Chapter 6
# Communication, intimacy and everything in between

When you and your partner are on the same page, marriage can be a very satisfying experience. However, when you both have problems, things can begin to get out of hand, and you start experiencing difficulties. You must make sure your marriage remains strong enough to stand the storms of life. This is where intimacy comes in to play.

## *Typical Interactions Between a Married Couple*

Well, this is the first thing that you need to know before we delve deeper into marital intimacy and sex. Let us take a step back to reflect on the days when you and your partner were dating. Do you recall the coffee dates and going to the movies? How about the sweetheart hung you had on each other's words? How was the experience? Is still the same with you? What happened?

Well, over time, you will realize that the newness you had with each other begins to wear off. That

91

is when you notice that conversations that were considered meaningful at first become more and less intentional and rather accidental.

One thing that is important to note is that as our lives get busier, we get caught up in the habit of doing a drive-by chat. In other words, your partner sends you a text to pick up the laundry or pass by the grocery store for something or what's set for dinner, among others. Then when you meet at home, the quick conversations continue.

Interesting enough, as kids begin to flurry around, you catch up at work and come home only to crash on the couch. Ask yourself whether this is enough. What changed? Do you feel closer to your spouse anymore? Is there anything you can do to build a closer relationship with your partner? We will talk about this in the next sections; keep reading!

*Does it matter what you talk about?*

Well, this is one of the questions most married couples ask after a couple of years in marriage. According to research, there is evidence that shows married couples spend some of their time in a day talking. Interestingly, this does not mean that they are necessarily engaging in a conversation that draws them closer to each other. It does not mean that these conversations contribute to their physical or emotional intimacy.

It is important to bear in mind that building a truly deep relationship calls for intentional conversations that come from and penetrates deep into the heart. In other words, if you want to be intimately close to your spouse like you used to be when you were dating, you have to have conversations every day that are much more than a recap of the things that went down during the day. Committing to having a purposeful conversation with your spouse enhances your physical desire for each other.

## *What is intimacy anyway?*

Before we can delve deeper into the role of intimacy in marriage, we must understand that there is a big difference between intimacy and sex. Often, you hear people using these two terms interchangeably, which is inaccurate. The truth is that you can be intimate with someone without necessarily having sexual intercourse. On the other hand, you can have a fantastic sexual relationship with someone without really being intimate.

Understand that intimacy is all about being open with your spouse without fear of being vulnerable. Concerning marriage, intimacy is more about being very close to your partner. Are you intimate with your spouse? Do you have a mind-blowing sexual relationship you're your partner?

The truth is, some people love each so deeply but then have difficulty establishing an intimate connection with each other. The main reason for this is that you do not allow your partner to be so close to you. It could be because you are shy. This can also be a problem that is coming from your partner.

### *How do you feel comfortable around your partner?*

Are you looking for intimacy with your spouse? If this is what you want, then you must be comfortable when around them. When you have a fear of being yourself when around them, this will only prevent you from achieving a deeper connection. You may be self-conscious about certain things, and that is perfectly normal.

There is nothing wrong to be careful about how people perceive you. But think about it this way, you loosen up a little, strengthen your marriage with your partner and you start feeling incredibly comfortable around them, sounds great right?

Are there things that you feel ashamed of doing before your spouse? At the beginning of your relationship, you may have been uncomfortable letting your partner look at you when naked or even without makeup. However, this changed over time. What happened?

When a relationship grows deeper, it feels less threatening to reveal your flaws to your partner. Some of us have found out that the things we perceived as flaws became the things that our spouses love the most about us. The truth is, relationships evolve, and over time, they turn into very beautiful parts of our lives that define who we are.

Realize that, when you are comfortable enough to do anything around your spouse is a brilliant thing. I mean, comfortable enough to shower while your partner watches you. Comfortable enough to use the restroom when your partner is in the bathroom. When you can show your bodies to each other without any fear, then you know that you are walking into a deeper level of physical and emotional intimacy.

This is when you get used to the fact that you are not always going to be your best. Therefore, when you are around each other in all situations, with time, everything comes to you naturally.

My partner and I like to think that we have achieved a high level of intimacy. At first, we could not take showers together, but with time, we did, and it's amazing! You should give it a try! However, understand that there are people who need a little more space but then are comfortable with their spouse from an emotional point of view. The most important thing is for you to make each other feel comfortable, make life as happy as it can be, and feel natural living together.

Ask yourself whether you feel comfortable around your spouse. Can you shower together? Can you stand him look at you without makeup? Can you spend all Sunday afternoon naked with your partner alone in the house? Think of anything that you feel uncomfortable with and start addressing it.

If you have anxiety or body image issues, it is high time you address this and let your partner journey through your fears with you. Your spouse is supposed to be there to encourage you and ensure that you feel loved, no matter what.

You could also seek professional help in dealing with negative body image issues so that you can enjoy greater intimacy with your spouse to the fullest.

### How does communication contribute to greater physical intimacy?

Have you ever looked over to your partner from across the room and you feel so much love in your heart that you walked up to them and kissed them? If not, then you need to work on your emotional connection. It is this kind of connection that only can be achieved through intentional communication with each other.

Understand that expressing yourself through physical means goes a long way in strengthening your bond with your spouse. It is a natural feeling that can only be achieved if you are emotionally close to your spouse. Remember that physical intimacy is much more than sexual intercourse. In other words, it is an an-all-day love affair that happens between two people who have a connection both at a mental and physical level.

There are times when we get lazy in our marriages as far as showing our spouses that we love them dearly by employing non-sexual affection. The more you hold a hand, snuggle, hug, kiss, and play stupid games together, with the more you strengthen your physical intimacy. So, what are you still waiting for?

You must start working on making your marriage feel like a real partnership. One of the ways you can do this is by ensuring that you are always present for your partner through good and bad times. When you achieve a good level of intimacy with your spouse, talking to them about sensitive subjects will come easy to you. In fact, the stereotypes that underlie intimacy issues of men having trouble being open and honest with their spouses will go out the window.

Having a solid marriage makes it easy for one to feel like they can rely on their spouse whenever they need their shoulder. You will come home when you have had a rough day and talk about it and be close to your partner without feeling ashamed even though you might have been on the wrong. It is such a beautiful thing knowing that someone has your back no matter what.

Understand that communication will not always be easy. There will always be times when you feel that you cannot communicate your feelings effectively. You are not alone. This is something that gets the best of us married couples, especially when we have a different personality to the person we married. If your spouse is someone outgoing and boisterous, your subdued personality may have a hard time keeping up sometimes.

What does this do to your intimacy? Well, the truth is, this might negatively affect your intimacy with your spouse. The main reason for this is because you may feel like you are always several steps behind, and your partner is miles ahead of you. In such a situation, the most outgoing spouse needs to recognize where their partner is at and try to compromise so that they can meet at a more neutral level. You have to learn how to communicate at all times with your spouse to effectively establish an intimate connection.

### *Is sex important?*

Now, it is high time we address the elephant in the room! Well, one of the questions I have heard so many people ask is whether sex is important and if it is everything. When it comes to cultivating a healthy marriage, you must bear in mind that sex is very important.

It is one thing to enjoy sex, and it is quite another to use it in predicting your relationship.

Sex is important, but it is not everything that glues your marriage together. It is there to help you connect with your partner and deepen that bond. When you enjoy sex regularly, your marriage becomes happy. In fact, it is an excellent way for you to show love and affection to your spouse.

Ask yourself whether you have enough sex with your spouse. How often do you have sex? Having a healthy sex life plays a central role in bringing wonders into marriage. Research shows that when you have regular sex with your spouse, the chances are that you will enjoy an overall better relationship in the long run.

When you and your spouse are satisfied both emotionally and sexually, it goes a long way in helping all other pieces of the puzzle into its rightful place. Taking good care of your family, kids and each other becomes easier when you both have a special time set apart for just the two of you.

Sex also goes a long way in helping you know that you are still attracted to each other. When you have been married for a few years, there is a tendency to worry about the wearing off of freshness in your union. They worry that the spark is gone and might not come back. You have children, and the next thing you know is that your body has changed and you don't know whether you will ever go back to how you used to be. You are worried that your partner will no longer find you attractive.

Despite all these changes, showing your spouse that you love them and desire them contributes to having a great marriage. It is the glue that will help you stay together and work towards achieving your couple's goals together.

Yes, there will be times when you will have sexual problems. Your sex life will evolve into something that you do not want. Then, there will be times when anxiety stands in the way of you exploring sexual intimacy with your partner. In such situations, you must try to address these problems before they ruin your marriage.

Realize that a good marriage is way stronger than sex. However, it might be difficult for your spouse to feel loved in this manner. This means that you have to seek professional or medical help fix your sexual intimacy issues. If you are not comfortable having sex, you should seek help from a professional therapist that has knowledge in this subject. Someone who can help journey with you through the problem so that you come out the other side successfully.

# Chapter 7
# How do you recognize a lack of emotional intimacy?

Emotional intimacy is an essential part of any successful relationship. It is how you are connected to your spouse. It takes openness and vulnerability for both of you to be close to each other. Without emotional intimacy, it can be difficult for couples to weather the storms that life throw at them.

Think of emotional intimacy as the glue that binds you and your spouse together. Once the initial excitements fizzle, you will still be able to overcome anything that threatens to break your marriage. But how do you know that your relationship lacks emotional intimacy?

Here are some of the red flags you need to look out for;

### *Sign 1 Feeling oddly distant from your spouse*

Have you ever felt that your partner is so distant from you and you cannot quite pinpoint what the problem is? You feel as though your partner's feelings are an arm's length away from you.

Well, the truth is that this is a sure sign of a lack of emotional intimacy. It makes you feel as though you are isolated from your partner. You do not spend time together anymore, and when you are together, you barely have anything to say to each other.

It is this kind of distance that signifies that your emotional intimacy is gone. It calls for you to act in rekindling the spark that you two had before. You must pay attention to ways in which you can both nourish and nurture your emotional intimacy so that it can enhance togetherness and a strong connection. Start by trying to ask and answer questions with your partner to see how things start growing from here.

### Sign 2 None of you talks about their emotional feelings

This shows that you do not have transparency in your marriage, indicating that you have not built a solid foundation of emotional intimacy in your relationship. In marriage, so many things happen, and you need to be able to come home and talk to your spouse about your feelings and emotions without fear of being judged.

Yes, it is not easy to open up and talk about your feelings, but in marriage, you should be able to talk to your partner transparently and with vulnerability. When you fail to talk about your emotional feelings, the chances are that they will bottle up to a point where they explode and become even more problematic. It can start showing through habits of arguing over small and meaningless things. It can be evident when you start stonewalling your spouse, among other ways.

When you lack the confidence and security to talk about your feelings with your spouse for fear of invalidation, it is indicative of serious emotional intimacy problems. It may not be easy to wake up one morning, build emotional intimacy, and go to bed in the evening having it. It takes time. But the most important thing is that you can start building it little by little, opening up yourself to your everyday fears, and within no time, you will start seeing changes.

### Sign 3 One of you sharing way more than the other does

Do you share more than your partner does? Is it the other way around? If one of you shares what they feel more than their spouse, then the chances are that there will be difficulty noticing when there is a lack of emotional intimacy. It may come off as one of you is a good listener. However, according to experts, this is an indication that there is an imbalance in your marriage.

In most cases, you will notice that the reason why you do not share more with your spouse as they do with you is that you do not feel comfortable expressing yourself openly. It could also mean that your partner is not creating a conducive environment for you to be open and vulnerable with them.

Therefore, when you realize that you are not opening up enough or your partner is not opening up enough with you, you must bring it up with them. This way, you both will work it out and find solutions that will help resolve the whole issue once and for all.

### Sign 4 You do not share your lives

When you keep physical distance from your spouse, this is an indication of a lack of emotional intimacy. It can be that you do not test them much, you do not go out on dates, do not share each other's experiences or just the mere fact that you lead completely separate lives although you live in the same house. This is something that is said to be harmful as far as your marriage is concerned.

When you lack emotional intimacy, the truth is that there will be nothing you share in common with your partner and hence have so little to nothing to talk about. A typical relationship is often characterized by long phone conversations, long texts, and long dates aimed at getting to know each other better. You can talk with your spouse for a very long time, and when you later think about it, you have no idea what you were talking about for such a very long time.

The truth is, it is a good thing that you should maintain long after you both are married. When this pattern disappears, it is a huge concern. It means that you are not sharing a fair amount of your life with your spouse. If you are not comfortable doing that, it indicates that there is an emotional distance between the two of you.

### *Sign 5 You do not touch much outside the bedroom*

As far as physical touch is concerned, there is a clear parallel between physical and emotional intimacy only that it may not be in the ways you think. Yes, behind the four walls of your bedroom, you may engage in physical touch and much more than that. But the trick is, are you able to maintain that even when you are not in the bedroom?

Can you kiss your spouse, hold hands, place your head on his chest when around other people? These are the small things that demonstrate an expression of emotional intimacy. According to experts, that comfortable physical closeness between you and your spouse requires a certain level of emotional closeness too.

In other words, what we see as the physical distance between the two of you is a reflection of what is happening in your emotional intimacy. When you and your partner have an emotional connection, it is shown in your physical connection. Therefore, if you do not touch much, then you have to loosen up, open up, and allow your spouse to come into your intimate space and experience it with you. Trust me; you wouldn't want to miss it for the world!

### *Sign 6 You no longer share hobbies like you used to*

Sharing hobbies with your partner is another aspect of balancing your emotional intimacy. When you stop doing things you love with each other, the truth is that your emotional connection begins to dissipate.

For instance, so many couples like watching Tv shows together and other times one of you takes one for the team just so that they can share the connection with their spouse. That is something amazing. However, when you stop focusing on what your spouse likes and enjoys doing, then you are checking out of emotional intimacy box.

Therefore, try as much as you can to build yourselves back up emotionally. You can start by selecting a new Tv series that you both can watch and enjoy together. You can even play puzzle games together or scrabble, among other things. Doing this goes a long way in creating space for you to connect and grow your emotional intimacy.

### Sign 7 Having trouble listening to your spouse

Even though you and your spouse share the same thoughts and feelings, emotional intimacy is not something that you build unless you both listen to each other very well. Understand that one of the essential signs that emotional intimacy is non-existent is your inability to listen to what your spouse has to say.

The fading of emotional intimacy is marked by you saying things that bother your spouse or are just completely tuned out of the conversation. This is something that you can observe both in conversations and other parts of your marriage. You do something wrong, and you do not care to apologize to your spouse for it.

One thing that you need to understand is that you can establish emotional intimacy by paying attention to what your spouse has to say. You listen carefully to their feelings and practice vulnerability with them. You demonstrate curiosity with what your spouse feels and experiences. In other words, you are willing to do all it takes to ensure that you connect with your spouse with compassion, empathy, and presence. Therefore, start by practicing active listening and loving communication with your partner to build and strengthen your emotional intimacy and connection with them.

### Sign 8 you are not seeking out each other's advice

When you are married, you and your spouse must support each other no matter what. However, this is hard to accomplish when none of you is seeking help and advice from the other. The truth is, no man is an island. You do not have everything figured out, and you need the counsel of your spouse to help you make important decisions.

Am not saying that you should dictate what your spouse should and should not do. However, you should start seeing your marriage as a place you can go and seek guidance. When you go seeking help from the rest of the world without first asking your spouse what they think, the truth is that there is no emotional intimacy in your relationship.

This indicates that you are not emotionally mature to seek your partner's counsel and support. You must conduct an assessment to determine whether this trepidation arises from your side or that of your partner. Then start opening up and let your spouse in whenever you need advice and support.

That said, it is important to note that emotional intimacy is a hallmark of a good marriage. When you lack it, then it means that you are both walking on the wrong track. With hard work, you both will be able to figure out your shortcomings and where you need help so that you can resolve every issue that arises. If it means going out on dates, signing up for couple's counseling, or having a heart-to-heart conversation, then you should be able to do it. You should always purpose to protect a good thing you have together. If you are meant to be together, then things will always work out that way.

# Chapter 8
# Increasing intimacy in your marriage

There are so many ways you can try to fix intimacy issues in your marriage. Most of these ways will need you to act and work on yourself. Start by recognizing that your marriage has intimacy issues that need fixing. To do this, you will need to employ the right communication channels with your spouse so that you can both work on improving.

In other instances, you will notice that it is challenging to try and fix intimacy issues in your marriage without bringing in a third-party. One thing that you need to note is that by seeking out professional help, you are giving your marriage a chance to be efficient. It may make you feel inadequate at first, but once all issues have been resolved, you will thank yourself for making that decision.

Here are some of the practical ways you can use to increase intimacy in your marriage;

## Experiment with "sensate focus" exercises

This is a very important form of foreplay that helps you focus on your partner while making love. It also goes a long way in enhancing your likelihood of achieving an orgasm. The secret here is for you to be a giver and your spouse the receiver. Your major role as the giver is for you to figure out various ways you can make your spouse feel good without necessarily having to resort to other go-to you normally use when having sex.

The trick here is for you to begin at the top of your spouse's head and then slowly work your way down their body using your fingertips. As you do that, roam around with your mouth and hands and anything else that strikes your fancy.

As the giver, it is your job to ensure that you incorporate a range of sensations so that the receiver can experience them with all their five common senses. Understand that the level of foreplay here focuses mainly on subtle aspects of sexuality to achieve true sensuality.

Even better, you can decide to build on this form of exercise at least once a month. Have sex without really using any of the positions that you normally use regularly. This way, you will spice things up and ideally discover some of the best positions and moves that turn your partner on as you go along.

We will delve deeper into sensate focus in the next chapter. You don't want to miss the action!

### *Make a game out of it*

One of the best ways in which you and your partner can try new things is by constructing a passion wheel. According to Ava Cadell, the founder of Loveology University, start by taking a piece of paper and then draw a circle in the middle of the paper.

Then go ahead and divide the paper into 12 equal pieces to create a pie chart. The next thing is for you and your partner to take turns writing romantic activity on each slice. This way, each one of you gets to fix at least six slices with the activities of their choice.

This can be anything you fancy from a bubble bath, watching porn, masturbating among others. Each one of you gets to pick one activity from the other's list one at a time as you take turns. This is one of the best ways to draw you closer to each other and enhance your emotional intimacy.

## Exchange three "love vows" each

Here, you must start by trying to figure out what your spouse wants more and then commit to doing it. Ensure that what you are committing to is something that you are comfortable doing. Such things may include promising your spouse 15 minutes of foreplay at least once a week. This goes a long way in helping you do the things you enjoy over time rather than letting them fade away.

Realize that these promises you are making to your spouse do not necessarily have to be physical. You can also make them be about meeting your spouse's emotional needs. For instance, you can commit to telling your spouse why you are grateful for your marriage at least once every week.

This is something that plays a significant role in eliminating creeping apathy or taking each other and your relationship for granted without really realizing it. The lack of gratitude is what is often referred to as an emotional black hole that eventually kills your spark and relationship.

## Check-in with each other each day

One thing that most people fail to realize is that

even though you spend hours of the day with that special someone, the chances are that you might still not have an emotional and intimate connection with them. However, it is not about the amount of time you spend with each other. The question is, how quality is that time together?

One thing that you can do is choose to spend at least 15 minutes every day sitting with your partner to catch up on how they are doing. Well, you may say that this is not sexy at all, and you are right. But the truth is, how many couples do you know that check in on each other every day? How many find this suggestion helpful in their romance life?

To you, it may sound so simple, but the truth is that it has the power to move your relationship to a higher level. It stirs up that feeling in your partner that you have invested time in keeping strong the bond you share even when life gets busy and chaotic. That got to count for something!

### *Get to know your partner on a deeper level*

How do you know your partner more than you already know about them? Someone might say that they already know all they need to know about their spouses, and there is nothing left to know. Well, to be precise, this is not true!

Start by asking each other questions that lead there. Some of the places you can draw your inspiration from are <u>The And</u>. This is a very cool interactive documentary whose main aim is to record couples asking each other questions such as "Do you think that am the best partner you have?" "Why is that?" "do you feel like we are living the dream we shared when we got married?" Once you have watched the video, this video shoots you at least 12 questions you and your partner can ask each other. If you want to keep playing the game, you can download the iOS app for just as little as $2.59.

You have to try this one; it's incredibly exciting!

### *Have one phone-free hour every day*

In this time and age, everyone seems to hold on to their phones, checking it every few minutes. On one level this is a good thing, but when it comes to spending time with your spouse, this can be a huge turn-off.

One thing that you need to understand is that the world will not come to an end if you just put away your phone for an hour to focus on the love of your life. I would advise that you take up this challenge and use it to your advantage.

Before the advent of phones and electronic gadgets, people were still able to stay connected for over hundreds of thousands of years. Cell phones just came a few decades ago, and we hang onto them like they are indispensable. To improve your intimacy, try to think through times when you and your partner often get distracted by technology. Is it when you are having a serious discussion together? Is it at the breakfast or dinner table?

Whatever time it is, make an agreement to both ditches your phones and computers for some time to focus on each other and having the good old-fashioned conversation with your spouse. You will be amazed at how much your affection for each other grows. Just try!

### *Engage in activities that helped you fall in love in the first place*

are there things that you and your spouse enjoyed when you first fell in love? Do you still do those things together? If not, then it is time to go on a rendezvous. Begin by making a list of all the things you both enjoyed doing together when you first fell in love and still take pleasure in doing them.

Well, as you move from feeling head over heels back into the present, the chances are that there are things that you allowed to fade into the past. It could be meandering through the city discovering hidden gems, cooking elaborate meals together, making small videos of yourselves making faces among others, it is high time you reintroduced them.

The truth is, you will fall in love with your partner all over again. Don't just sit there thinking that you will do those things later and then you forget all about them. You must aim to do them with your spouse at least once or twice a month. Think of it as a way to have a steady stream of dates with your partner that you can look forward to. Remember that feeling you used to have when waiting for those evening dates with him/her? I would not want to miss it one bit!

### *Try new things*

Try to identify some new exciting, terrifying, and exhilarating activities that you and your partner can engage in. When there is a mix of these feelings in those activities, the truth is that they will go a long way in enhancing your attachment to each other. You will realize that there are tons of things you have in common with your spouse that you had no idea existed, and that alone is enough to glue your relationship together.

If the activity is scary as though you are hitting a roller coaster, sampling an exotic cuisine or ziplining or skydiving, your body will release oxytocin, dopamine, or endorphins that will bond you and your partner together. When this is combined with that rush of adrenaline, your tummy will swoop in more ways than you can imagine.

### *Have sex like it is the last time*

When we first visited our therapist, she advised us to have sex like it was the last time. Yes, it is a tad morbid, but there is a reason why this is a piece of great advice she gave us. We took it, and we ran with it to the secret parts of our lives.

When she gave this to us, at first, it felt awkward. But what keeps ringing in your head is "what if this was the last time I ever make love?" What is it that you would do differently? When you begin to put this into perspective, you will snap out of la-la land and start focusing on every little detail of that magical experience.

Trust me; it makes the whole difference.

## Download the Kindu app

Some so many people are bored with their bedroom antics and feel shy about it. They do not know where to start broadening their horizons from. Well, I am here to give you good news; Kindu app. This is a free iOS and Google Play app that offers you access to a wide range of sexual ideas on your phone, which you can use to spice up things in the bedroom.

If you and your spouse like the idea, all you need to do is download it, and everything will show up as a match. If you're only you like it, then the other will never know. It's one of the safest ways to explore what you might be into, especially when you are both not ready to talk about things just yet.

## Make out, but don't let it go any further

I like to think of kissing as facial intercourse! It is one of the most intimate ways we can be as intimate as human beings. Unfortunately, it is one of those things that easily slip away when you have been with someone for a long time.

One thing that you need to note is that kissing is one of those good gestures you show affection to your partner and never goes out of fashion. Start by giving your spouse a small peck in the morning before heading to work. With time, you can start to up the ante into makeouts without sex just like you used to do when you were teenagers.

Hold the sex until hours later. This means you give your partner a clue about what it is that you are doing so that they do not get confused or hurt when you refuse to go all the way! This way, you both get a chance to build anticipation until when you are ready to hit the home run if you are picking what I am putting down.

# Chapter 9
# Steps to an epic sensate focus

Just like we have discussed in the previous chapter, this phenomenon is about touching and being touched. To maximize the potential of sensate focus, you must start without really having any preconceived notions of what you are likely to experience, how much pleasure you will enjoy, or how you will feel.

In other words, what you are doing is allowing yourself to have an open mind so that you avoid coloring your experience and feelings. Do not judge or evaluate to avoid being boxed in: was it ecstatic? Boring? Good? This can be self-defeating at its core because you will be put in the position of an observer instead of a participant. All you have to do is focus on what you are feeling physical. As you let your fingers run through your partner's body, feel their skin. Is it rough? Moist? Warm? Smooth? This way, you get to focus on the experience.

### Sensuality vs Sexuality

One of the things that is important to note is that

your sensuality is more superior than sexuality, and that is what you should be focusing on. No matter how aroused you are, it is critical that you do not cross the limits. When you are not required to touch the genitals, breasts, kiss or have intercourse, you should keep it at that; off!

It is this kind of prohibition that goes a long way in helping one pay a close attention on sensuality that comes with touching, as a distinct entity in its right. It also plays a central role in taking pressure off your spouse when responding to your touch in any way.

Additionally, it helps you discover and stay away from ingrained behavioral patterns. So many couples often consider the time spent on sensate focus to be useful and pleasant in awakening their sexual and sensual feelings. To achieve this, you have to ensure that you and your partner are well rested, relaxed and are kind to one another.

It is critical that you try as much as you can to emphasize on privacy as a way of eliminating distraction. Take at least 30-45 minutes practicing this exercise. Bear in mind that optimal nudity is key and hence the need to avoid getting in constricting clothing that will limit skin-to-skin contact with your partner.

## *Step 1 non-genital touching*

Ideally, when you are getting started on the sensate focus, both you and your partner should be undressed, showered, and free of all jewelry. You must designate one of you to be the giver and the other the receiver.

If you are the receiver, you must focus on the sensation you get while being touched. This means that you are not to reciprocate the touch at least for the moment. It is your role also to let the giver know when you are not comfortable, whether physically or psychologically.

Keep the touching going for at least 15 minutes, because when you are starting, it may feel unnatural. Therefore, the first few minutes is meant for getting over the strange feeling. It is also important that this does not prolong into boredom, something that will ruin the whole experience.

Some of the things that you need to consider during the touch include;

*Playing a texture awareness game*

As you touch your spouse's skin, and move from one part of the body to another, pay attention to the skin texture. Is there are away the texture compares between various parts of the body; neck, calves, back, and hands? Which skin do you feel is supple and silky?

*Vary the firmness and tempo of the touch*

The next thing is for you to feel the difference between a long-drawn-out touch, a quick one, and a slightly firmer touch. You must try to switch from the staccato rhythm so that you can employ a smoother and a more languorous touch. Do you feel that the changing tempo alters the sensation of your touch?

Try to compare the touch with fingertips and that of the whole hand. Is there are the difference when you touch with one hand and when you do it with both hands? Do you feel sexually aroused? If you do, you must avoid turning the exploration into a sexual encounter.

Additionally, either one of you can ask the other to end the touching session. If you both start falling asleep, then you can ask your partner to end and try another time when you are well-rested.

So, what is the point of the sensate focus?

Well, the truth is that you are not doing this for the sake of giving your spouse a massage. The point here is for you to experience a wide range of sensory experiences and take note of how they feel without necessarily getting distracted.

The second part of the exercise is about reversing roles. This means that you should try as much as you can not to end the session before you can switch roles. When you do reverse roles, you must avoid comparing the touching styles. You do not have to employ the same approach as your partner. Remember that you are two different people with distinct perceptions, feelings, and instincts.

Yes, some couples prefer repeating what their partner did for a couple of days. However, what is interesting is that they notice something different each time. This means that you can try out a wide range of techniques, timings, and variations so that you can experiment with them without feeling that you are under pressure. Remember that this is not a test to pass before graduating onto the next level.

## *Step 2 Incorporate breast and genital touching*

The second step is to take the exploration to the next level; breasts and genitals. Here, you are not to kiss or engage in sexual intercourse. The guidance here is the same as in the first step; nudity, cleanliness, and privacy.

To get started, it is also important that you designate who will be the giver and who is on the receiving end. For the receiver, you should start by lying on a flat surface with your face down to help facilitate the process. Even though the "ban" on touching the genitals and breasts have been listed here, the giver mustn't alter the manner of overall touch.

The point is to ensure that you are not turned on or make something happen for your spouse. Instead, you have to focus on your sensations as far as exploring your spouse's body is concerned. If the sexual touch is overwhelmingly tempting, it is advisable to take a step back to reflect on what you learned in the first step.

Slow things down and start feeling the curves on your spouse's back. Compare that to the contour of their hips. Start tracing the edge of their spine and try to compare how it feels to the soft tissues on their upper arms.

Now, run your fingers through their hair as if your intention is to feel the texture, length, and thickness. Once you are comfortable and flowing in the rhythm of the moment while connecting with the sensation registering through your fingertips, begin to shift your spouse to a new position.

Place a few pillows behind your back so that you lean your back as though against the wall while sitting with your legs spread on the bed to achieve a V-shape. Position your spouse (receiver) in between your legs so that their back is against your chest. Ensure that when you reach down to your spouse, you can touch most parts of their body.

At this point, as you keep up with the general exploration of your spouse's body, throw in a new twist to add into your non-verbal communication (the receiver placing a hand on the toucher to explore). The main aim of hand riding is not for your partner on the receiving end to take over but instead to help transmit information to the giver in a manner that is not goal-oriented. However, the receiver has a chance to offer the giver with non-verbal feedback of what they prefer subtly.

Although the teacher's role is not to anticipate

feedback from the receiver, giving responses to silent messages goes a long way in ensuring that the receiver's reactions are incorporated. With this technique, the receiver can guide the giver on where they like a firm touch for the toucher to linger there for a while.

It is not that the receiver is criticizing the toucher's technique, rather it is about asking them to try something they both might like. As you touch the breasts and the genitals, remember not to change the touch for a sexual experience. In other words, when touching these places, it is critical that you are brief in and around them and then move on to other parts of your spouse's body. You can return to the genitals and breasts as part of a natural ebb and flow of the touching experience.

As you do this, your spouse might get sexually excited, and you mustn't direct your focus on genital stimulation. If your spouse wants to get more genital touching, either one of you can provide stroking to guide the firmness and tempo of the touch. When you start feeling as though the touch is becoming obligatory, then it is high time you stop.

Here are some pointers that you need to keep in mind;

Always feel free to move to positions different from what your partner suggests

If you are the receiver, then you must give your spouse pointers on where you would like to be touched and how to be touched especially when in the genitals to avoid guessing on what you prefer.

At this point, ensure that you stay away from kissing as this might push you into cruise control as far as sexual and sensual behavior is concerned. The point here is for you to break old patterns rather than trying to make them solid.

If on the receiving end, you are aroused enough to orgasm, it is fine to allow the orgasm to happen. However, this is different from making it happen. Just like in the first step, there is no limit on how long you take here. However, do not linger too long into boredom. Also, ensure that both of you experience the roles before moving on.

### *Step 3 Add some lotion*

This is one of the best ways you can add in some sensory awareness. Notice that when you add some lotion, the dimension becomes silkier and slicker. You should use a non-alcoholic lotion that is hypoallergenic. In most cases, baby oil will do the trick.

You can try warming the container of your lotion in a basin of warm water before you use it. Try as much as possible to avoid dripping the lotion onto your partner's body. Pour the lotion onto your arms and rub it to warm it up before you can apply it on their skin.

Some couples like their touching experience without lotion and then introduce it along the way. If this is you, it is perfectly okay. On the other hand, if you also like to experiment by using it on the one hand and not the other so that you can compare and contrast the sensation, you are welcome to do so. Some use the lotion from the very beginning to the end, and that too is fine. Whatever approach you choose to use, do not drift away from the whole point of the exercise: focusing on the sensation.

### *Step 4 Move on to mutual touching*

In this step, you are beginning to extend your scope of touch by getting rid of the artificial switch between you and your spouse. Here, each one of you has the freedom to use their newly improved skill set on sensory awareness to pay attention to their fingertip sensations and physical sensations simultaneously.

However, you must keep refraining from kissing or having sexual intercourse. Bear in mind that what you are trying to achieve here is the addition of a whole new dimension of sensuality into your marriage. If you become too sexual rather than sensual, it is fine if you lie back and allow your body to do the touching for just a few minutes. You can also switch your attention from more sexual areas to less sexual ones.

Additionally, you must stay away from sexual fantasies when engaging in this exercise. Well, I do not mean oral sex per se; what am referring to here is using your lips and tongue as a way of sensually exploring your partner's body. The truth is, there is a huge difference between the two intentions.

Have you engaged in oral sex before? If you have, try approaching it from a sensual manner and note the difference. The other variation worth trying is trying to change the scene of your sensate focus say from the bed to the couch or the shower among others that you prefer. This way, you get an opportunity to alter your feelings and perceptions into rather interesting adventures.

## *Step 5 Sensual intercourse*

The moment you have all been waiting for is finally here! Here, what you are doing is extending the awareness of your physical sensation into having genital contact with your partner. Bear in mind that the main goal here is to uncover what you both consider interesting and pleasurable.

Begin this exercise with non-genital touching. Bring yourselves into a rhythm while you stay aware of what the fingertips are trying to tell you. Do not worry about getting aroused. Slowly extend the scope of your touch to include the genitals and the breasts. Do not shy away from using your hands to rise through your body as you guide your spouse on what you would like. However, try not to direct every move. Once you are both comfortable, you can slowly slide into a position that allows you to get into the cookie jar! But do not get in just yet, hold it there!

Here, start using the principle of sensate focus that you have employed from the very first step but this time extending the touch to the genitals and breasts. Try as much as you can to explore all sensations of rubbing and touching. Here, both of you are active participants: no more receiver and giver roles. Take note of the sensations you both experience from touching each other.

If at this point, intercourse is desirable, begin with partial penetration. Slide-in slowly and take your time to focus on the sensations you get; warmth and contact. Hold it there for a few seconds. Can you feel any difference? Now, slowly withdraw for a minute before you resume intercourse.

Once you have tried these sensual variations, you can go deeper and also faster. Some couples enjoy is slower while others like it faster. Others like it shallower while others like a deep thrust. As you enjoy each other, try to focus on sensations as you give yourself a chance to enjoy a new way of making love to your partner. If you find this pleasurable and would like to employ it from time to time, talk to your partner about it. Remember, the whole point is for you to communicate your desires and feelings, something that is key to achieving healthy sexuality and sensuality.

# One last word

After all, is said, one thing that you need to bear in mind is that a good marriage thrives on openness when it comes to sharing your beliefs, emotions, and desires. Communication is indeed considered the most satisfying aspect of any marriage relationship.

Most marriages indeed go through their fair share of rough patches that can change how couples communicate with each other. So many couples begin to develop bad habits that give rise to destructive patterns when things are not moving smoothly and on the right track.

You will hear people in troubled marriages saying "we just don't talk anymore" What they mean to say is that they do not effectively communicate with each other. The truth is, couples are communicating with each other all the time. Even when you are giving your partner that silent treatment, you are communicating.

Just as a summary, there are five major pathways of communication in marriage; the context of the situation, spoken/written communication, emotions, nonverbal cues, and touch; all of which we have touched on in this book.

Well, it is very easy for a couple to focus on just words as a form of communication. However, the truth is that this only forms a fraction of communication a couple of share regularly. If you are going to streamline communication in your marriage, you will have to be willing to look at all the pathways of communication. Look out for all the red flags and address them with your partner. If you must, seek professional help from experts.

Indeed, communication is a very complex concept than we can wrap our heads around. It is even more challenging to juggle up all pieces of information you get from your spouse. When you are calm, you must take time to reflect on your fights with your spouse. What are the different types of information you give your spouse when fighting? Is there something that you can learn from your fights? Is there something that you can do differently?

Better still, you can take time to have a chat with your spouse when both of you are calm to talk about the gaps in your communication and how you both contribute to these gaps. Try to find solutions to address these gaps together. When you try to resolve communication breakdown issues together, you are both opening a whole new level of understanding of the issues you are both facing.

Just remember to keep learning ways to get it right each time and how you can communicate better so that your marriage can move in the right direction.

So, what is it going to be for you this year? What do you intend to do differently as far as your communication with your spouse is concerned? The time to rekindle that spark is now.

Don't waste the chance you have been given.

© **written by: Katerina Griffith**

# Book Description

Are you married or hoping to get married soon? Do you wonder how couples manage to live together for the rest of their lives? Do you want to build a strong and long-lasting relationship with your spouse/partner?

Well, don't worry because we have you covered!

When you are just starting a relationship, you probably feel the jitters when planning the outfit to wear for dinner with your partner or even when composing a text message to them. You want that vibe at the beginning of your relationship to stay right throughout your relationship.

One thing you need to understand is that building a strong, healthy, and long-lasting relationship is not a walk in the park. It takes so much awareness, diligence, and being present in the relationship. It takes honesty and keeping an open mind to live a "happily ever after" with your spouse. But does this always happen? Do all couples that get into a relationship enjoy a strong and long-lasting relationship?

Not!

Here, we will discuss;

- What marriage is all about
- The secrets to a long-lasting relationship with your partner
- The steps to take when building a strong and long-term relationship
- Marriage and Parenting
- Romance and everything in between
- Marriage and In-laws
- Marriage and money
- Divorce-proofing your marriage

For this and much more, you can position yourself for a "till death do us part" relationship. It will not hurt to give these tips a try, and who knows, this might be what you have been waiting for all these years.

So, what are you still waiting for?

Come with me and let's start building your marriage one brick at a time!

# Introduction

While the term marriage is very familiar to us, most people do not understand what marriage is. Well, today, we have people secretly moving in together and calling that a marriage. The truth is marriage is a relationship in which two people make their union official, public, and permanent. It is about taking vows to create a bond between you and your spouse until death do you apart.

While it is easy to take vows and promise each other heaven on earth, marriage, as they say, is not a bed of roses. Every day, you hear of people getting a divorce, what happened to their vows? What happened to the "for better and for worse" promises?

One thing that is important to note is that every marriage comes with so many challenges, and in most cases, very profound ones. How you choose to manage these challenges with your spouse will determine whether your marriage comes crumbling down or stays firm. The truth is that it is not an easy task. It takes a lot of commitment to guard the love that you have with each other. It means that you have to jettison lots of misguided beliefs and habits that you have carried with you for so many years.

To build a strong marriage means that you have to take key measures that will divorce-proof your relationship. This means that each one of you in the relationship identifies and shores up several strengths and then reinforce them with new skill sets and techniques that will play a role in helping you share your lives.

Throughout your relationship, there are lots of things that happen. Your personalities change, romantic love waxes, bodies change, in-laws get involved, and children come with parenting requirements. Each one of you has dreams of their own that they would like to achieve in life. Then there are dreams that you both share as a couple and would like to accomplish them as well. All these in one lifetime!

The truth is, no marriage if conflict-free!

It is important to note that what enables a marriage to endure the test of time is how they choose to handle conflicts. Take a minute to ask yourself how you and your partner deal with problems whenever they arise? Do you go to bed angry at each other? Do you bring in other people into your issues as a couple? What are some of the things you do to keep the spark alive?

This brings me to the next most important thing; finding the right spouse for you! This is a personal decision that is very important in determining how long and how strong you keep the relationship working. Yes, no one can indeed see into their romantic futures. But the science of relationships and marriage offers a deeper insight into making that decision.

When you make a commitment to marry your partner, some of the things you need to ask yourself is whether he/she is the right one for you, how you know that they are the perfect spouse for you, what makes you think that you will enjoy the rest of your life with them, is the timing right? Knowing what matters most when making this decision is very critical in building a strong and long-lasting relationship.

No one wants to get married, and the next week, they are getting a divorce during their honeymoon. But the bitter truth is that whether or not marriage makes sense depends ultimately on the traits of an individual you are uniting within holy matrimony.

You have to realize that the fact that you are

getting into marriage or are already married someone does mean that your life is not about you alone. This is something that you have to understand that you both are married, and the marriage is not about you. When I was getting married to my wife, I said in my rehearsal dinner speech that "Our marriage is not about me, and it is not about us."

Everyone laughed because they must have thought that I was cracking a joke. Think about all the guests that have traveled all across the horizon to witness you and your partner get joined in holy matrimony. You must think, "our marriage is so special," right?

What you need to understand is that your marriage with your spouse is not just about the two of you. The vows that you made or are making in front of hundreds of thousands of friends, family, acquittances, and colleagues should be the guiding force for your union.

While I am not a marriage expert, getting married to my spouse has been a learning curve for us since the first day, we said: "I do." I do not have any authority to tell you how to live your life or how to drive your marriage. But the one thing I know for sure is that my marriage is not about me, and so should you if you are looking to build a healthy and long-lasting relationship.

In the true sense of a wedding, the vows involve you and your partner. You both take time to promise each other love and respect for the rest of your lives together. You promise to be true to one another. That is something that you can only give your spouse and them to you. What you are simply doing is making a commitment to take your partner's life into your own hands and accepting the responsibility for each action you take that affects them. Your marriage will change you, shape you, and form you together.

But is that all marriage is to us? If it is, then the truth is that you are missing out on something truly beautiful about marriage. You may be wondering why I even said that marriage is not about me or us. Realize that you both had a ceremony and invited so many people to attend and witness the beautiful union that you and your spouse were starting. If it were just about the two of you, why would you even bother to have a public ceremony? There would be no need for friends, family, priests, and sacraments, right?

How we treat our marriage ceremony should tell you that it is far higher than the two of you. IT is so important that you have to involve community participation. On the other hand, for most of us, it is about bringing in life to the world.

The first thing that comes to mind when you think of bringing life is having children and watching them grow into young, successful, and holistic individuals. While that is bringing life into the world, it is only one way of doing it. It is the most simplistic way of thinking about the concept of life-giving. Showing the words how we love each other is one way of bringing life. The way you live in marriage with your spouse should be in such a way that you lift one another and the people around you. You are there to change the world together by the way you live and love each other.

What is important to note is that when you are living your marital vows to the very best of your abilities, the love, honor, and commitment you have with each other pours and spreads into the world. Our marriage to each other is what changes us, and it is our responsibility to change the world positively. When your purpose of building each other up and use the grace you have been freely given, you bring so much light and hope into others' lives.

During our wedding ceremony, my wife and I shared the Holy Eucharist and gave the body of Christ to the congregation. This was a symbol for us to remind ourselves and the guests at all times that the act of marriage was not of self-love alone but of offering ourselves for service to others. That is exactly the marriage I hope to carry with me for the rest of my life. As my spouse and I grow in hope and love, we purpose to find various ways we can bring life to the people around us. We purpose to serve the people around us uniquely.

Indeed, this is something that will help us nurture a strong, healthy, and long-lasting relationship with each other. The good news is that we don't have to do it alone. God equips us with all we need for us to do what He has asked of us, and that is exactly why you should never think that your marriage is just about the two of you.

# Chapter 1- The Marriage Basics

*"Success in marriage does not come merely through finding the right mate, but through being the right mate."*

– Barnett R. Brickner

A year back, my family and I embraced a minimalist lifestyle. There was so much clutter in our home that took up so much time, energy, space, and money. When we started cleaning out the things that we did not need, we got rid of many non-essential items that were eating up too much space in the house. This was one of the best decisions we had made in a long time.

We noticed that a whole new world started opening up. We started finding space for the things that mattress to us most. The things that we valued most. Because of that, we spend lots of time at the dinner table, a playroom for the children and get out more for picnics and walks with the family.

When you get rid of non-essential things in your life, you get more room to focus on what is essential and have found that this where true life lies.

In the same way, marriage follows a similar path.

When you are just getting married, you have nothing but each other. This is the point where you focus on the most important building blocks of marriage so that your relationship is not only solid, but also healthy and long-lasting. However, as your relationship continues to grow and expand, lots of stuff accumulates and becomes a distraction from what is truly essential.

Soon, you stop looking at the value of the relationship, and you focus more on the value of the home. We start saving for retirement and children's college funds that we forget to pay attention to the health of our marriage. We spend lots of time in the garage taking care of the car that we forget to spend time in bed with the one we love.

This is what I refer to as clutter. They first steal your family's attention, then money and time. What is left is very little that the marriage cannot stand strong and begins to crumble down one building block at a time.

You must wise up and start realizing that material things will not help your marriage stay strong and long-lasting. Your home, car, and retirement account can be very nice, but you don't need them to make your marriage a success. Here are essential building blocks you need to cultivate in your marriage;

## Love and Commitment

This is the core of your marriage. When you choose to love your partner and marry them, what you are saying is that you are committing to taking them into your life. Love and commitment are traits that go far beyond fleeting emotions portrayed in the movies, romance novels, and big screen TV series.

Realize that feelings will come and go, but what will stay forever is your decision to commit to each other until the end of times. This is precisely what defines a healthy, strong, and long-lasting marriage.

Note that marriage is a life-long decision you make to commit to each other despite the thick and thins that life throws at us. It is true that when things are going well, your commitment to stick by each other is easy. The true test of marriage is displayed when you choose to remain committed to each other through all the trials of life. That is what we refer to as True Love!

## Sexual faithfulness

This is something that most people do not quite understand its true meaning. When you talk about sexual faithfulness, it goes beyond our bodies as couples. It involves what we see with our eyes, mind, soul, and heart. When you get married to your spouse, everything you have is theirs and should not be shared with anyone else.

This means that you cannot have sexual fantasies about someone other than your spouse. Marriage means sacrificing all your sexual faithfulness and fantasies to your partner alone. When you choose to offer moments of sexual intimacy to anyone other than your spouse, you are sacrificing your sexual faithfulness to them.

To build a strong marriage, you must guard your sexuality daily. You have to devote it to your spouse alone. To be sexually faithful to your spouse, you must cultivate a sense of self-discipline and awareness of what consequences you will face if you did the contrary. Choose to resist putting anything before your eyes, body, and heart that will compromise your faithfulness to your spouse.

## Humility

The truth is that no one is perfect in this world. We all have flaws and weaknesses. What is even more interesting is that relationships reveal these flaws and weaknesses faster than any other institution on earth. One of the most important building blocks of a strong and healthy marriage is the ability to admit that you are far from being perfect. Accept that you make mistakes and that you need forgiveness.

When you choose to hold an attitude of being superior to your spouse, you are inviting resentment into your relationship. This is exactly what will stand in the way of a long-lasting marriage.

Do you sometimes look down upon your partner? Do you think that you are more important than they are? If you are a victim of this, you need to take a step back and find where you went wrong. Go back to the crossroads and find your way back. Take a pen and write down all the things you love about your spouse. This exercise will help you stay humble. Do this as often as you can, and you will keep your marriage in check!

## Patience and Forgiveness

Based on the fact that no one is perfect, it is always important that a marriage is built on patience and forgiveness. Getting into marriage with your partner means that two very different people are choosing to come together to be joined as one thing! Does it mean that you both have similar beliefs and values? Does it mean that you both will like how your partner does things?

Definitely Not!

It is about accommodating your spouse and learning ways to show them unending forgives and patience. It is about choosing to admit with humility when you are wrong and stop expecting that your partner is perfect. It is choosing to let go of past mistakes and faults rather than holding your partner hostage.

You cannot build a long-lasting relationship if every time there is a mistake that is made, you see revenge. If you keep holding on to past hurt, you are never going to focus your effort on what is best for your relationship. Today, choose to let go of your partner's past mistakes and forgive them. Forgiveness is the best way you are going to set your heart free and your relationship free, healthy, and happy.

## Time

There is no way you are going to do your marriage work if you don't invest time in it. You have to realize that this is something that has never happened and will never see the light of day.

A successful relationship requires that you become intentional in your actions and invest quality time with your partner. The truth is, when you have no quantity time, it can be hard to have quality time.

Realize that the relationship you have with your partner is one that requires intimacy. It is a deep relationship that requires you to have your whole being invested in it, and that includes your time.

While there are so many responsibilities we have outside our marriage, it is important to note when all else is lost, the one place you go back is home. This means that you have to look for ways you can make spending time with your spouse. Do date nights, picnics, and coffee dates with them every often. This is how you stay in each other's lives.

## Honesty and trust

This is another building block of a strong marriage. However, unlike all the other building blocks we have discussed, trust and honesty are the essential factors that you need to cultivate on an ongoing basis.

One thing that you need to realize is that building trust in a relationship takes time. You can choose to be selfless, patient, committed, and faithful, but trust is something that you have to nurture over time. It can take weeks, months, or years to have it. It starts with you being yourself and doing the things you said you would do.

Because it takes time, you better get started now!

If you need to rebuild your trust in a relationship, you must start working even harder than you have before.

## Communication

When you are in a healthy marriage, it means that you communicate effectively and openly with your spouse as much as possible. You openly discuss finances, parenting, and intimacy with each other. However, you don't stop at that;

you go as far as communicating with each other what your dreams, fears, desires, and hopes are. You not only share the changes that your kids are going through but also changes taking place in your hearts and souls.

Realize that having honest and forthright communication with your spouse is the key foundation to a strong, healthy, and long-lasting marriage. Being married means, you are both joined together into one thing. Therefore, stop keeping secrets from your other-self. Start communicating openly and without judgment with your spouse and watch how your bond grows stronger than you have ever imagined.

## Selflessness

Even though this is a trait that will never show up on any marriage survey, the truth is that most marriages are broken because of selfishness. Most studies will hide it in finances, infidelity, lack of commitment, and even incompatibility, but the bottom line is selfishness. The reason why you choose to cheat on your spouse is that you only care about your feelings and not what your partner will feel.

The truth is that when you are selfish, you only care about you and you alone. That is why instead of choosing to forgive your spouse, you resent them and lack patience with them.

Today, I will challenge you to give your hopes, dreams, anxieties, fears, and life to your partner. Start living life together. This is a very simple call for you to start valuing your marriage and your partner. Instead of resenting them, choose to accept them, and be patient with them. Care for them and invest you're all in them daily.

Trust me; when you do what I am asking you to do, you will see the worth in it at the end of the day. Remember that a successful, healthy, and strong relationship is more important than all the temporal material things people tend to focus on. And this is something that will last longer even when all else is gone!

# Chapter 2 - Types
# of relationships that last longer

Is there a way to know if your relationship will last? Do you know if it was meant to be? if you are still dating, is there a way to know whether if it is "the one?"

Well, all these are questions that we have all asked ourselves at one point in life. Some people are still in a dilemma today about their relationships. They are wondering whether it will stand the tests of time. It would be lovely if there was a definite way to predict with accuracy that your relationship will be strong, healthy, happy, and long-lasting. But the truth is, there is no one way to tell for sure.

Look around you, family, coworkers, and friends; there are so many of them that are cynical about love. No one can blame them for being cynical because all the statistics out there concerning relationships are very grim. Everyone is getting into a relationship, wondering whether it is the one. Our commitments are not fully from the heart. We choose to put in one foot and the other outside in case things don't work out for the both of you.

One thing you need to realize is that your relationship cannot be successful if you get in with doubts. Realize that the success of your relationship depends on the choices that you make today. You have to believe that yours will beat the odds. Contrary to what most people have made you think in the past, your relationship can last more than you give it credit for.

A study conducted in 2012 showed evidence that over 40% of couples who had been married for over a decade were still deeply in love with each other. The same study also showed that about 40% of female participants and 34% male participants who had been married for over three decades were still deeply in love with each other.

The truth is, every relationship we get in is a risk. We are not sure whether it will last, but we allow our hearts and minds to guide us to the one we want to spend the rest of our lives with. The good news is that there are various types of relationships and signs that each type carries that indicate success and long-lasting unions. These types are;

## Relationships that are shared around forgiveness

As we have already mentioned, conflicts are bound to happen in a relationship one time or the other. How you deal with them will determine whether yours will stand the test of time or not. When you fight with your spouse, how can you tell if you will be able to address the issues at hand in an amicable manner?

Well, the truth is that a strong relationship will not seek to reduce conflict. This is mainly because there will always be conflict in any relationship, and there is nothing you can do to prevent that from ever happening. When you choose a partner, the fact is that you chose a certain set of problems. They come as a package!

If you are looking for a partner that you will never have to fight with, get mad at, or even complain about, then you will never find one, at least not in this world. While it is often difficult to believe, fighting in a relationship is good. According to research, it is evident that a couple that does not fight at least three years into the relationship is indicative of an unhealthy marriage.

A healthy relationship is one that is stable but

also has a healthy conflict. Arguing with your spouse is not a sign that you are destined for doom. Understand that this is all healthy and normal. The trick is for you to focus on addressing the problem instead of attacking each other. Once you resolve the issue, you choose to forget each other for the parts you contributed and move on.

According to a marriage therapist, Jeanette Raymond, the true measure of a strong relationship is how fast you resolve issues and reunite. If you are looking to cultivate a strong, happy, and long-lasting marriage, then you have to be willing always to take the initiative to have each other's back and embrace one another even when you have a difference of opinion or disagreements.

My wife and I have made it a rule that even when we disagree, we have to resolve our issues before going to bed. No one signed up to spend their night on the couch. We address our issues and go to bed, talking to each other.

But what do you do if there are poor conflicts in your relationship?

The truth is, this is a sign that your relationship is unhealthy. That said, you must make a choice not to stay angry with your spouse after fighting. One mistake I have seen couples make is hold a grudge even long after the disagreements have been infused. Others choose to sweep issues under the carpet instead of addressing them head-on. What is even worse is that other couples freeze their emotions and completely shut down as though the rest of the world does not exist.

You must work with your spouse to rebuild the emotional connection that you once had together. Make it a commitment to restore security into your relationship. You can do this by first ensuring that you override your hurt feelings. Choose to be happy rather than being right. When you hold a grudge against your partner, you are simply choosing to breed resentment that will eventually destroy your marriage.

Understand that it is not about what you are fighting about; it is how you choose to fight!

## Relationships based on adventure

If there is anything that often stands in the way of lasting relationships is boredom. We have all seen couples get married with all the fire in their bellies. They cannot keep their hands off each other. However, a couple of years down the line, they can't stand the sight of each other. They get into these grey areas where everything seems to be predictable, uninteresting, repetitive, and boring to death!

Why is that?

So many things come and distract them from paying attention to each other. We have careers, children, and side hustles that make life a real tough nut to crack, and we get so busy chasing goals that we forget to stay connected with our spouses.

But how can you stop this from happening?

According to research, there is evidence that couples who enjoy an intense love and a strong bond with each other are those who enjoy taking part in challenging activities together. They love going on an adventure with each other. It is these new adventures that often are arousing and stimulate the brown into interpreting it as an attraction for your spouse. This is what reignites that spark that you had when you first fell in love.

If you want to shake things up, going on new adventures is the best place to start. The truth is that with new experiences, you activate the reward system in the brain, and you have a release of feel-good hormones, dopamine, and norepinephrine.

Stay open to new activities!

## Relationships built around intimacy

According to research, couples who are unhappy with their sex life often have a tough strain in their relationship that has a high chance of ending in a split. If you are thriving for a strong relationship, you must aim at cultivating a good sex life.

The truth is, sex is not everything in a relationship, but it is something! In fact, the more you have sex, the more you want it every day. On the contrary, if you have less sex, the lower the likelihood of you wanting it. And this finally contributes to a loose connection between you and your spouse.

When you have sex, you stimulate such hormones as oxytocin often referred to as the bonding hormone. Research indicates that happy couples have sex at least 74 times annually. How many times do you have sex?

If you are below this number, aim for more and more sex! Trust me; your marriage is counting on it!

If you are worried that you do not have enough sex, notice that intimacy is not all about sex, though you can use more of it (just saying...). Start by building your intimacy with your spouse in such ways as touching, cuddling, holding hands, extending each other a loving eye contact, kissing, and hugging, among others. Everything else will come naturally! (if you know what I mean...)

## A relationship built on trust

As we have already mentioned, if there is anything important in a relationship is trust. It takes time to build trust, and when you have this, you know that you are up for a long-lasting relationship. If you lack trust in your relationship, then it becomes difficult to maintain a strong bond between the two of you.

Take a look at yourself in the relationship, do you think that your partner can rely on you? Do you think that they can count on you on anything? Are you trustworthy? Do you hide stuff from your spouse? Do you cheat on your spouse behind their back? Do you have feelings that you are trying to hide from your partner?

Realize that strong relationships take trust, and that is not achieved by keeping secrets.

Rather than choosing to focus on small things and nitpicking mistakes that your partner has made, choose to look at the big things. If you have anything that you are keeping from your spouse, it's time you start letting the cat out of the basket.

If you don't trust your spouse, then you will never believe in a strong union together.

## Relationships built around a shared future together

A long-lasting relationship, in most cases, is about sharing dreams and goals with your partner. It is about seeing your future as a place where you both are the major players. It is about both of you sharing values and goals before you can even get into a relationship with each other.

A survey interviewed couples who had been married for over 40 years. What this survey revealed is that sharing core interests, values, and a general outlook of life with your partner will often go a long way in stacking the odds in your favor. Research conducted in 2009 showed that couples who are happy in their marriage often share similar personalities.

Don't get caught up in what the movies say; opposites attract each other. Trust me, a good percentage of couples with different personalities often find their relationship stimulating only if it is kept short-term.

But what if you are not certain of what your relationship goals are?

Well, one thing you need to understand is that common goals often work together and make your lives work together harmoniously. You can start working on this with your part. Start by finding out what you both consider as your couple goals, whether you would like to start a family together, if you plan to own a house, how many children you would consider ideal for the both of you, among others. It is these common goals that go a long way in strengthening your relationship.

However, if by any chance it ever crosses your mind that you wouldn't want to start a life with your partner, then probably it is time for you to start moving on.

## Relationships based on shared vulnerabilities

At one point in your life, you must have heard someone that was scared of falling in love, or maybe you did. There are so many reasons for this, and one of the most common ones is fear of commitment. In other words, you feel vulnerable.

The thing is, several people, wish to be in a relationship, but then they don't know how to open up to their partner when they are hurt. They feel vulnerable often because they fear that if they opened up, they would be rejected. We often feel that if our partner finds out that we are anything less than perfect, strong, or intelligent, they will walk away. They will stop liking us.

Let me tell you something; you cannot build a healthy relationship without feeling vulnerable. Think of vulnerability as the glue that binds the two of you together. Knowing that someone loves you the way you are and for who you are is the ultimate gift you can get from a relationship. On the other hand, loving your partner for who they are is also one of the most fulfilling experiences you can get from life.

Realize that when you choose to fear

168

vulnerability, you are choosing to sabotage yourself. It is this kind of fear that will stand in the way of you giving your all into your marriage.

But maybe you are wondering how you could know if your partner will embrace your vulnerabilities. Well, you can find that for yourself. If you are afraid of vulnerabilities, the chances are that you will feel the need not to expose your personality to your partner. You may feel that keeping a distance from them makes you feel safe and in control. In other instances, you may feel embarrassed to share your true feelings with them.

Whatever it is, note that vulnerability is often thought of as a sign of weakness, but in fact, it is a strength. Trust me, no one is born comfortable in their skin. However, it takes so much strength, self-confidence, and character to show your vulnerability to someone else. If your partner is genuine, then they will respect you for allowing them to see the real you. Putting your vulnerability out in the open is something truly attractive, and only honest people can appreciate others' authenticity and imperfections.

If your partner does not see it, then he or she does not deserve you!

That said, having a strong, healthy, and long-lasting relationship is really what you make. You have to start by being committed to your relationship. Let no one lie to you that the grass is always greener on the other side. If there is anything that kills relationships is comparing ourselves to the people around us. There will be couples who are beautiful than us or happier than we are.

The truth is that a happy couple will not look at what others have and compare it to what they have. Having a happy marriage is about being satisfied with the view of your door. Therefore, invest time and effort into making your relationship what you dream is right for both of you, and you will eventually have it.

# Chapter 3 - The marriage secrets

When it comes to getting married, there are only a few people who are certain what they are getting themselves into. The truth is that we all have an idea of what marriage is about. What we have are hopes, expectations, and dreams of what marriage truly looks like. When we watch some of the movies starts we like, we think that the kind of marriages they show on Tv is what it is like in real life.

Well, let me tell you something, you have no idea what marriage is until you are there!

When I was getting married to my wife, there are things that I thought I knew, but once I got in, that is when I got the real deal! Getting married does not also mean that you will know everything. However, you will get to learn new things as you get by.

Here are some of the secrets I can tell you will strengthen your marriage if you pay attention to them;

## Secret 1 Marriage is more about intimacy than sex

If you ask anyone that is single and planning to get married what marriage is about, they will tell you it is about sex. While there is so much value you draw from getting married to your partner as far as your sexual relationship, the truth is that a good marriage is built on intimacy. This is the only way you are going to enjoy good sex and not the other way around.

When I got married, I was excited that we were finally going to enjoy all the sex we want with my partner, and we do! However, I never quite understood the concept of real intimacy until I committed to spending the rest of my life with my lovely wife. What I have come to learn and understand is that marriage is a brilliant opportunity in which you allow your partner to look right inside your life, heart, and mind. That is what true intimacy is about!

## Secret 2 Marriage uncovers self-centeredness but also cultivates selflessness

Confessions, I didn't realize how selfish I was until I got married to my wife. One year down the line, my selfishness was out in the light. I could choose what restaurant we would eat, who gets to clean up, what movie we will watch, and who gets the remote. What was even shocking was that each time we argued, my wife would apologize first even if I was the one at fault.

One thing you need to realize about marriage is that if you are going to make it last, you have to learn to place the needs of your spouse before your own. This is how you start learning the true meaning of being selfless. Trust me, even though this is a hard lesson to learn, it is a beautiful reminder of God's selflessness when He gave His all so that you and I can have it all in abundance.

## Secret 3 Oneness means being ONE

Have you taken a moment to think about the spiritual and physical benefits of oneness? The truth is that most people fail to consider the part where it is slightly inconveniencing, living in one house, sleeping on one bed, sharing the same bathroom, working with the same budget, and operating one bank account, among others.

The truth is, when we get into marriage, we stop being "me" and become "us." We stop having things that are "mine," and we view everything as "ours." To build a healthy relationship, you have to care for everything as though they were

173

not just yours but also belonged to the person that you love most.

## Secret 4 At certain points, you will be disappointed

This is one of the most difficult realities that most couples find it hard to believe. You must be aware of your spouse's humanity and yours too. However, it is interesting that this reality does not hit home sooner until you are disappointed.

My wife and I have always loved each other deeply. This does not mean that we have not hurt each other a few times in our relationship. One thing you need to bear in mind is that when you marry someone, you are choosing to bury your heart in theirs, and theirs in yours.

What you need to be prepared for is that there will come a day when you will feel an ache. This hurt can come in the form of an unkind word, a selfish moment, or even a thoughtless action. However, you must choose to embrace the grace of God so that every hurt and wound pave the way for forgiveness and restoration. Each wound should serve as a constant reminder of our need to love deeply and better each time.

## Secret 5 You must learn the meaning of forgiveness whether you like it or not

The fact that you are going to get hurt means that you have to embrace the reality of learning the essence of forgiveness. One lesson that you must learn is that forgiveness comes not just because your partner deserves it, but because it whelms from a heart that understands how much forgiveness we had received even when we least deserved it.

## Secret 6 Marriage will cost you

When you are in the glory of marriage, the truth is that you will lose a part of yourself. In other words, you exchange a portion of who you are for the sake of taking up a little bit of who your partner is. In short, you learn the essence of giving and taking. In marriage, you learn to let go of the things that do not matter to you at all. What you realize eventually is that what you have given is far much less than what you receive ultimately.

Trust me; love is good, just like that!

## Secret 7 Love is a series of decision and not a feeling

Before you got married, the chances are that you did not understand the strong feelings that you felt. And then, suddenly, you start realizing that you cannot trust your feelings because there are days when you don't like your spouse, and most days, you just can't let him go.

Note that feelings are temporary. They come and go. They are more like a compass, and in other instances, they serve as a guide, but the truth is that you cannot follow them because they don't lead anywhere specific.

The true test of love is what you do when you feel that you don't like your spouse. Understand that marriage is about choosing to love your partner even when you don't want to. You are choosing to give your all into serving them because you committed to them, the world, and God that you would love them "for better or for worse." It is about you constantly choosing your spouse instead of yourself.

That is what true life means!

## Secret 8 Marriage requires that you learn how to communicate

We have mentioned before that one of the most important building blocks of marriage is effective, clear, and honest communication with each other. It does not matter what it is that you are fighting about with your spouse. What matters the most is what you would do about it. How will you choose to communicate to them how you feel.

In short, marriage is about you constantly communicating with your spouse, your values, beliefs, opinions, and feelings. It is about not fearing to ask the tough questions, tell the hard truth, or even respond to difficult questions. It serves as a lifeline between you and your spouse. Trust me; there is no other way around it. You have to be ready to take responsibility for what you say, how you say it, and how you react to your partner's response.

Watch your tone, sarcasm, and body language! It speaks a lot.

## Secret 9 Marriage is not the end of your destination

When you are still dating, it is often easy to look at marriage as your grand finale! It is that thing that you have been dreaming about since you were a little girl or boy. It is what you have lived for all your life, and finally, it is here. The next thing you think of when you get married is, "Now what?"

What you need to understand is that the relationship and marriage God has blessed you with is just a small portion of the grand scheme he has set for your life. The truth is that your purpose and passion will supersede the relationship you have with your partner. God will use your relationship and the love between you and your spouse for the glory of His name. Your marriage is not the end of everything. Instead, it is just the beginning of the many more blessings he has in store for you.

So, quit giving up and fixing your mind on an ending. He has so much up his sleeve, and you have not seen anything yet!

## Secret 10 Marriage offers you a glimpse of so much more

Apart from the fact that you already know God has so much more in store for you, there is a lot you have to learn about God as you interact with other people regularly. Realize that there is a reason why God uses the institution of marriage when talking about the love He has for the church.

There is no single relationship you are going to have that will compare to that intimacy that is exchanged through marriage here on earth. The love that God has for us is magnified through the lens of a strong, healthy, and long-lasting marriage. But the best part is that he uses the institution of marriage to teach us, shape us, refine us, and put us through the test. In other words, it is through marriage that God keeps making us be more of Him.

When we reflect on the love of God in the way we love our spouse, we honor Him, and that is exactly what He uses to keep our marriages alive. What you need to understand is that there are so many ways you can achieve holiness, and marriage is one of them. Note that you are a different person because of the relationship he has given you and realize that he is not yet finished with you. Always purpose to expect from Him every single day.

# Chapter 4 - Steps on how to build a strong and long-lasting relationship

Once you have said your vows, you and your spouse go for your honeymoon. For most marriages, the honeymoon period has a shelf life. But the question is, "does this mean that you can no longer have those fluttery butterfly feelings of anticipation after the honeymoon?"

The precise answer here is; Absolutely Not!

The truth is that all marriages go through rough patches, and unfortunately, some are not able to survive this and come out the other side alive. However, some do!

So, what is the secret to their survival?

Here are some of the steps you can employ to cultivate a strong, healthy and long-lasting relationship;

**Step 1 Always appreciate your partner**

Once you have been married for a couple of

years, that passionate kiss you used to give your partner before they leave for work in the morning can easily change into a simple peck on the cheek. That soon changes from a peck that pays attention to your partner to barely lifting your head off the computer screen.

I have been married to my wife for over two decades now. And, there are times when I have felt as though we have become familiar with each other that we were settling for routine stuff. This is something that you probably identify with, and what you need to realize is that it is a real danger to your relationship.

According to research, almost 50% of the men that have cheated on their spouses blamed their behavior on emotional dissatisfaction. This is not about sex! The truth is that when a man starts feeling that his connection to his wife is not appreciated. They begin to become vulnerable to advances they get from other attractive women that keep listing for them. This works the other way too!

The truth is, every relationship is like a shark. It has to keep moving forward or else it will die. You better keep making progress in your relationship, or else things will dry up.

## Step 2 Be grateful for the little things

Over the years that I have been married, I am guilty of keeping scores with my wife. There are times when I have calculated who has done what, how, and when. "I cooked last night, I cleaned the children's closet last and so it is your turn to clean the house." Hell, even claimed that I initiated sex last time and so it was her turn now.

You probably have done the same too.

I will tell you something for sure; playing tit for tat in marriage is childish. The danger in doing this is that it keeps chipping away your connection and trust with each other little by little.

If you must keep scores, at least keep scores of the positive things that your partner does for you each day. Take a moment to appreciate them for what they do and let them know how special their actions make you feel. Trust me, when you embrace gratitude, your partner will soon be inclined to do the same.

## Step 3 Practice honestly even when you are ashamed

Have you maxed out the credit card and are trying to hide the bills? Trust me, whatever it is that you are doing and trying to keep it a secret from your spouse, it soon turns back and bites you in the ass.

At one point, you will be applying for a home loan or even talking about budgets, expenditure, and vacations, and these money issues will eventually come out in the open. This is what credit reports are all about, remember?

What you need to understand is the fact that while infidelity often happens in bed, it also applies to finances. If you choose to walk down this road, realize that you are giving away the trust that your spouse has for you. It is not just about money or sex. It also applies to your feelings and connection to your spouse. If you feel that something has changed, you must say it.

Trust me; I have personally learned this lesson the hard way. Do not allow communication issues to fester for weeks or even months. Just a small thing you keep from your spouse might mean years of marriage counseling and trying to win over the trust that you had built on each other from the very beginning. It will take a third party and investing lots of money and time to get your marriage back on track. If you quit telling yourself that things will get better and realize that they could get even worse, you will just come clean with your spouse and dodge a bullet! Just do the right thing!

## Step 4 Take care of your looks

When you first met your spouse, they probably were very beautiful or handsome. You loved the way they dressed and how they smelt. While that was not the only reason they fell in love with you, that made the whole difference.

Once you are married, it is very easy to get caught up with the hustles and bustles of everyday activities that you don't even pay attention to the way you look. You let your appearance to slide just like that.

Take a minute to think about when you first met your partner, would you have walked around with your hair shabby and teeth not brushed? Would you have your PJs on in front of your guests?

My guess; NO!

Well, don't get me wrong. I am not saying that you look like Oprah Winfrey each time you are getting ready for a night of TV series that you both love. There are far too many couples that have transformed from Dan to Roseanne Conner or Cliff to Clair Huxtable. Neglecting your appearance has dangerous repercussions as far as relationships go.

Observe good grooming and dress up for your spouse. From time to time, dress up for nothing at all. There are times when I walk out the door for a boys club, and my wife is like, "Honey, you look and smell nice." The least you can do is to pay your spouse the same courtesy of looking good to them like you do when you are heading out with your boys or girlfriends.

## Step 5 Foster relationships outside your marriage

I have been going for boy trips since I have been married, and so has my wife. Even though we have children, we still have those nights that we spend away from the family with friends. When you foster relationships away from your marriage, you open yourself to learning from others' experiences and stories. When you get away from your spouse, you get to call each other and start those romantic conversations you used to have when you were dating.

While your relationship needs to be the primary one, it does not have to be the only one.

## Step 6 Watch your words

The bible tells us that a wise woman will keep her home if she watches her tongue. The tongue is a very small organ, yet the most dangerous one. With just one nasty and unkind word, you can destroy a lifelong relationship. You never tell your spouse that your neighbor is attractive, that's a first!

Never start your conversations with, "You know what your problem has always been?" This is the last thing you ever want to hear from your spouse. Hopefully, you already have a good sense of yourself at this point in your relationship and know that saying such things will just put your relationship in jeopardy.

If you are angry, hold back all the things that you can say to your spouse out of anger. Take a walk or tell your spouse that you will talk about everything later. Don't say something that you will not be able to take back. Before you utter a word, think about it; is it true, is it kind and is it necessary? If it passes through these three gates, then you can go ahead and say it. If not, then don't say anything!

## Step 7 Put away the jumper cables yourself.

When it comes to family, there are big things and then there are little ones. Big things in this case may include;

- Draining your savings account so that you can satisfy your gambling habits
- Forgetting to mention that you have another family stashed somewhere in Brooklyn
- Living under a false identity because you are a wanted criminal in another state

These and more are some of the recipes for divorce.

The good news is that not so many people face problems of this magnitude. In most cases, the problems that we mostly suffer are repeated and petty annoyances, which with bottled anger over time, it eventually explodes. These small issues are like your spouse borrowing a jumper cable from your car and forgets to give them back.

These are the things that lead to anger and

MARRIAGE ADVICE SELF-HELP BOOKS

unkind utterances that eventually brews resentment. The danger of leaving such small things unaddressed is the fact that they slowly tear us apart. Instead of bottling up anger, choose to address them as soon as they happen. Simply ask your spouse right there and then if they finished using the jumper cables and put them back in your car. If they had forgotten, they will do it right away and everyone is happy!

Do you think you can do that? Your relationship is counting on you!

## Step 8 Relish the silence

Did you know that some of the best ways you can address some problems is to walk away? This is especially the case when you are boiling in anger. Trust me, not every single issue needs a remark or you addressing it right there and then. The truth is, not every insult is intentional.

This is why you need to practice how to let something go once and for all. Learn how to forgive your spouse more and then forget about what happened in the past. Let the past stay in the past so that your focus is on what lies ahead of you. My grandmother always told us, "sometimes you have to bite your tongue until it hurts and bleeds!"

Remember that this is the person that you married and there was a reason why you did that; Love. Act like it!

With silence, what you are doing is not condoning the problem, but choosing to let it pass. When you keep your cool but then harbor bad thoughts, then the truth is that you are breeding disease. Take care of you for you. If it is bad for someone else, it is definitely bad for you too.

## Step 9 Recognize the ebb-and-flow

It is only death that is flat-lined. It is true that life is full of ups and downs, mountains and valleys. This same analogy applies in marriage. Think about it from a second, if you lost your partner today, would you be happy?

It is absolutely unimaginable, right?

Truth is, living without our spouses is something that will bring tears and sorrow. There are times when maybe your spouse has been sick and we could not stand to see them go through pain. Then there are times when we are so mad at them that the last person you want to spend the night with is them. We have all been there.

Realize that relationships too come with so much ups and downs. In marriage, most of the time you feel as though you are on an emotional battlefield. It is not birds chirping outside or the kind of poison you are considering putting in their food. The battlefield here is not watching a couple across at the restaurant eating their food without even talking to each other. These people have already reached the flat-line. They just don't know it or are still in denial about it!

The battle field here is when months turn into years and you definitely know what the reaction will be even before you say anything. It is when the book you just completed reading last night suddenly is on his/her side of the bed. In other words, it is all the ebb-and-flow that you both go throw every day without the waves.

## Step 10 Be kind

In most cases, you will realize that couples tend to take advantage of each other maybe because they know that they are loved by them. They know that they can easily get away with anything. For instance, when you have a bad day at the office, you come home and then take it out on your partner as if they did you wrong.

We all have been victims of that at some point in

our relationships.

But does that make it right? The fact that your spouse understands that you must be having a bad day, does lashing out on them for things they have no idea about make it right just because they are your spouse?

Definitely Not!

It is important that each morning you get out of bed, you ask yourself what it is that you will do for your partner that day to make them happier. When you actually mean it, you will build your relationship for the better. You will come home each evening irrespective of how the day was knowing that even when the world around you is crumbling down, there is just one person that can make you smile and you can do the same for them. You come home and leave all the worries, fear, anger and anxieties out the door and walk in to the love of your love for a beautiful evening full of love.

## Step 11 Maintain passion and intimacy, in and outside your bedroom

As I have already mentioned earlier, intimacy is not just about sex. Passion on the other hand is not just about doing it on the kitchen counter.

In short, do not allow the status quo to define what healthy and normal sex should look like. Understand that things often change over time but that does not mean that you should stop having fun. Realize that intimacy is a song that comes in so many dance moves. It can be through cuddling or even conversations. Create ways to embrace all that and more with your spouse. Spice things up and don't confine yourself behind four walls. You can do it even in the open...Just be careful not to do it in the public! Because that would be a crime.

# Chapter 5 - Marriage and Parenting

## The Relationship between Marriage and Parenting

Parenting is a game-changer to all marriages. In many ways, it can change the relationship dynamic for the better or worse, depending on the specific set of circumstances. In television commercials featuring baby-shower cards, diapers, and a litany of baby products, parenting, and marriage are depicted as pure bliss and effortless. Your relatives will sell you a story about how babies are a heaven-sent bundle of happiness – and they are – but they skip the hard work that goes into making it all work!

Of course, it is essential to love our children. But it is crucial to be alive to what parenting does to marriages. There is no reason that loving your child and working on your marriage should be mutually exclusive. A happy marriage almost always means a happy baby. Marriage happiness, sustainability, and worth are liked at the hip with parenting.

Studies into the relationship between marriage and parenting indicate that most relationships change for the worse when couples transition into families. Initially, caring for the baby means sleepless nights, a surge in demands in bringing up the baby, and an abundance of new expectations on both parents. The parents also have to hold down the requirements of a job. Between 30 and 50 percent of couples that become parents face massive stress and depression.

University of California, Berkeley researchers, establishes that more than 70 percent of all new mothers faced a marked decline in their marital satisfaction. Around one-third of new mothers and fathers experience substantial depression after becoming parenting. One-eighth of all couples that transition into parents experience divorce by the time their babies hit 18 months.

Shifting from lovers to parents can be tumultuous to your marriage. The transition shakes the foundations of your relations. The result is massive disruption of the normal flow of information between partners. It also upends the status quo of emotions and individual responsibilities. In short, there is a learning curve for the lovers when they become parents. Completing the learning and adjusting accordingly is vital to the success of parenting and marriage.

The emotional disruption is mainly driven by the changes in the typical social dynamics. For example, a working mom's life shifts from the bubbly office colleagues for breastfeeding, dealing with mountains of laundry, and bottle-washing. After around six months, she faces the prospect of changing back to her working routine. The husband has to work with the wife through the entire process. However, most fathers feel left out of the early years of caring for the child. The overall result is each of the spouses is doing more, the communication lines and frequency declines, and both feel massively underappreciated.

As the kid grows, you suddenly find yourself wondering about your child will be enrolled in the right preschool program. You worry whether your daughter or son is in the right music, art, and tumbling tots' classes.

## Can Parenting be used to Strength Marriages?

It is not easy. It is difficult. But marriage can be used to sweeten your marriage, make it stronger, and long-lasting! Most people view parenting as a collection of stressors that will make your life miserable and probably accelerate the end of your relationship with your spouse. However, with the right touch, parenting can be the glue that holds you together. In this regard, it will benefit your relationship as well as the wellbeing of the kid(s).

All you can do to leverage parenting in improving your relationship within a marriage is to put your relationship first. Recognizing that your marriage is a work in progress goes a long way to cementing your commitment towards bolstering your bonds. Working on your differences consistently also helps strengthen the foundations of your relationship while ironing out disagreements before they become more significant issues.

A focus on appreciating each other while minimizing criticism is essential in sweetening your relationship. Communication is the underlying foundation of a relationship. Maintaining the bidirectional flow of information, opinions, views, and perspectives are necessary, retaining the enthusiasm to sustain a relationship of married spouses with a kid(s).

Using parenting as a tool to improve your

relationship quality and sustainability needs a deliberate effort targeting the dynamics of parenting. Understanding the expected disruptions to the relationship parenting brings will help you be better prepared. It also means that you are better equipped to harness the parenting changes and making them work for your relationship.

Learning about parenting and preparing for the shifts it brings should include both spouses. This process must be collaborative firstly because both of you will need the knowledge and skills to maneuver through the impending changes. Secondly, a concerted approach is likely to succeed in maintaining a working and effective relationship. When both of you put in the work, you are susceptible to shoulder the burden equitably. Although parenting cannot biologically be equitable, it creates a sense that the husband is supportive of the wife during this period.

The challenge facing most couples going into marriage is that they are not prepared for the disruptions of parenting. They are not ready for the upending of their lives they face after the baby is born, and parenting begins. As a result, parenting becomes overwhelming, physically, and emotionally. This leads to a surge in conflicts and an increase in the likelihood of divorce or unhappy marriages/relationships.

Here are some suggestions on how you can use parenting as a platform to build a stronger and long-lasting relationship and marriage:

### *Talk about the Certainties and Uncertainties Ahead*

Talking about uncertainties does not make them any more confident. However, it will help you be emotionally prepared and sure of yourself when navigating through the moments and circumstances of parenting.

It is also important to plan and ventilate some of the particular issues, such as splitting errands and household chores. It is essential to talk about where the income of the family will come from. In this case, it is crucial to answering the following questions: who is going to be the breadwinner? And who is going to stay at home rearing the child?

Talk about the day-care option. Establish who will get your baby to the day-care center and who will get him/her back. Explore the issue of a babysitter, the budget for this option, and plan your lives around what you agree. Figure out how night shift duties will be split, who is going to wash or sterilize the breast pump and bottles daily. Figure out the shopping schedule, cooking plan, and cleaning chores.

These details seem small and harmless. But without figuring out the division of labor regarding these aspects, they might contribute to frustration, stress, and depression. If left unsorted, they can gnaw away at the relationship.

However, figuring them out creates an understanding and collaborative approach that is healthy for your relationship. It also establishes a sense that everyone is doing their fair share. Moreover, developing a concise plan on dealing with these chores and duties reduces the chances that you will be overwhelmed as a couple when parenting begins. Emotionally, you will be prepared for the deluge of tasks and responsibilities, which will make it markedly more comfortable to handle and transition into the parenting role.

### *Focus on the Downside of Parenthood with the View of Avoiding its Pitfalls on the Marriage*

Maintaining a positive and hopeful perception of

parenting is important for new fathers and mothers. But it is vital to guard against lofty expectations that will be shattered by the reality of fatherhood and motherhood.

Yes, babies offer massive joy, and they bring a lot of happiness to a marriage. They also carry an uptick in physical and emotional exertions that can take their toll on the relationship. Bathing the baby, feeding, entertaining, and changing the baby 24 hours a day and 7 hours a week are demanding chores. All couples should be emotionally and physically prepared for such demands before they begin their roles as parents.

Focusing on and talking about the downside(s) of parenting is essential in marriage. It will help you to cope with the changes and disruptions to your lives. It is okay to talk about your fatigue, frustrations, and even anger with your spouse. Ensure, to be honest with your partner regarding these issues and also maintaining a supportive stance.

Feeling anger, frustration, and fatigue does not mean that you are a terrible parent. It is crucial to admit these emotions and focus on working together to resolve them within the marriage. This approach helps in disarming these emotions and thus prevents them from negatively affecting your relationship.

For example, you can agree in advance that if one of you is overwhelmed and is unable to fulfill their chores, the other will cover and take care of the baby for a while. This provides an option of relief for the overwhelmed partner. It also establishes a mutually supportive dynamic that deepens your affection for each other in the midst of a challenging period.

Fatigue, frustrations, and even anger resulting from anger can marinate into more significant issues within the marriage. For example, these emotions can easily lead to resentment of each other, lack of trust, and a breakdown in communication. By focusing on constant and honest communication, you will always know how your partner is feeling at all times. You can render your support when they need it and shoulder some of their fear and uncertainty.

### *Maintain Honesty about Gains and Losses*

In many instances, parenting will lead to some gains and losses. For example, you have gained the baby of your dreams. He/she melts your heart every time you see them. However, you

201

cannot avoid feeling sad and empty because of the loss of your typical sex life. For the mother, you lost your sleek pre-baby size 8s and replaced them with elastic-waist jeans.

Most new parents typically complain, silently, about the disruption to their lives occasioned by the baby and their parenting duties and responsibilities. These complaints and silent resentment cause the marital distance to widen. In some extreme instances, it can lead to shame and a decline in self-esteem.

For example, a new daddy might feel replaced by the baby in his spouse's life and affection. The mother might be frustrated and even sad about the ways parenting (pregnancy, nursing, and the rigors of childcare) have transformed her body. These feelings are normal among new parents.

Sharing such feelings of loss, shame, or disruption is vital in dealing with the emotional toll of parenting. Maintaining honesty about these issues with your partner helps you to feel better and strengthen your bond as a couple.

Communication regarding these feelings helps establish a perspective for behavior. For example, feelings of loss might make the mother snappy and frustrated, which might spill over to her interactions with other people, including the husband. The husband might also display emotions and reactions that are out of the norm.

Through communication and honesty, you will sort through these emotions and explain the context of behavior. The resulting understanding will create rigor room for a learning curve and some space for the growth and development of your relationship.

## *Avoid Apportioning Blame for Marital Blips*

Through experience, the first baby is the biggest and most dynamic challenge your marriage will ever face. Both of you will experience massive exhaustion. Additionally, you will be dealing with a shift in your identities, roles, and new expectations. Moreover, you will face an enormous decline in the time for personal pleasures to non-existent.

The solution to this myriad of challenging circumstances for parents is – do not feel responsibility or guilt for the decline in marital happiness. Additionally, do not blame your partner either for this eventuality. However, your duty will lie in not doing anything to turn this situation around for both you.

Eliminating blame from the parenting process allows both of you to take stock of what has happened, understand the core changes you face, and device ways to address the emerging challenges.

Without blaming your partner, it is easier to work through any of the challenges you face. However, with blame, your partners might shutdown or apportion some blame, which will lead to a cessation of communication.

By being honest about the changes you face as a coupled due to parenting, you establish a platform upon which you can build solutions. Although parenting brings changes, they can be addressed through adjustment, collaboration, and hard work.

### *Redefining Parenting or Co-Parenting*

Parenting is a universal phenomenon. However, the specifics of this process differ from one family to another and from one couple to another. In most cases, couples establish a relationship dynamic that influences parenting. At the same time, the parenting approach adopted by a couple affects their underlying relationship and marriage as a whole.

Partners that maintain admiration, support, and agreeableness with each other's parenting styles when bringing up their kid(s) are likely to have a happy, durable, and long-lasting marriage. The link between parenting style and marriage happiness is indicative of the role parenting plays in sweetening a marriage and bolstering its sustainability.

The exact dynamics in every marriage are determined by the relationship dynamics, cultural constructs, social issues, economic factors, and other internal and external aspects. A couple must take deliberate efforts to define the elements of engagement within their relationship regarding parenting.

Well-defined parenting processes can help breath a new life into a relationship and marriage as a whole. It also prepares the couple for the issues they will confront as parents, which differ markedly from the aspects they faced before they had a child.

It is essential to understand that having a good marriage before a child arrives does not necessarily mean that such a marriage will remain steady when parenting begins. Marriage partners that are parents operate under a new set of rules as you judge each other's parenting styles, approaches, and abilities.

The solution to this challenge is to seek out and admire everything that you can about your partner's parenting style and approach. Reach out and seek a supportive and understanding conversation about the aspects of their parenting that you disagree with. For example, some of the areas that parents disagree n include rewards versus punishment, discipline, meals, TV time, and bedtime.

Such conversations are designed to reduce the sharpness of disagreement, bolster the ability for compromise and agreement, and help marry the two parenting approaches into a comprehensive one that complements both the mother's and father's plans.

While this ultimately helps the upbringing of the baby, it also reduces the points of friction between the parents. It also helps bring the partners closer and bolsters marriage strength and sustainability.

### *Cultivate a Support Network*

Exchanging notes and experiences with other parents with children the same ages as yours will offer massive emotional support. It also provides reassurance of what you are doing, especially when navigating the challenges of change, disruption, fatigue, frustration, and even anger.

Sharing with other parents helps understand that, however wrong or awkward it gets, it is probably healthy. Such a perspective is vital in dealing with challenges, especially the overwhelming type. The frequency and vigor with which you blame your marriage, yourself and your partner for the problems you face will reduce.

You are also more likely to focus on finding solutions to the challenges you face. Sharing will also bring a feel-good aspect into your marriage and the things you do together.

Typically, it is easier for moms to find support groups compared to dads. Moms can easily access such groups by interacting with other women with babies through mothers' groups. Moms can also meet at pediatricians' offices, kids' playgrounds, or children's activity groups. In many cases, dads have reduced opportunities to access to other fathers.

Moreover, you can gather friends, family, and neighbors will to help with some of the chores within the family, such as cleaning, meals, errands, and childcare. Such help can help reduce the pressure on you and your spouse. Therefore, this will allow for an improvement of emotions and the bonds between the two of you.

Overall, parenting introduces a new dimension into the married life. Typically, this can help strengthen the bond between the married couple or drive them apart. To help build a strong and long-lasting marriage, parenting should be embraced as a massive challenge that needs exhaustive emotional and physical preparation. At the same time, couples should be alive to the unpredictable and dynamic nature of parenting. In this regard, no amount of effort will thoroughly prepare you for parenting.

However, being emotionally prepared and physically braced, as a couple, will go a long way. A collaborative, communicative, and accommodating approach to parenting by a couple will not only mitigate any challenges they will face, but it will help build a stronger and sustainable marriage.

# Chapter 6 - Romance And Everything In Between

A commitment of unconditional love is the widely accepted description and definition of marriage. This vivid portrayal also captures the underlying driving force of a happy and long-lasting marriage – romance.

Romance is the outward portrayal, expression, and demonstration of love. Therefore, the intensity, frequency, and sustenance are a surefire thermometer to establish the position and strength of your relationship. Romance is also a sure indication of the contentment of partners within a relationship.

In marriage, the traditional expectations of a family driven by culture and conventions are involved in gauging and influencing the relationship. However, romance still retains its crucial role as the glue that nourishes relationships and keeps them going even during rocky times.

In building and sustaining a marriage, there is a need to cultivate oneness and bolster intimacy. You and your partner have to be committed to meet each other's emotional and physical needs.

Marriage faces significant dynamism and changes. Marriage partners might fail to hold high levels of commitment at all times. As a result, there is a need for a

problem-solving approach. When the relationship hits trouble, there is a need for a way to find a solution. In the second or third year of marriage, something typically happens in most marriages. The romantic heat that warmed the relationship before marriage dies down somewhat. The decline of romance leads to a plummeting of the ability of these partners to meet each other's physical and emotional needs. This increases the chances of conflict and the likelihood of divorce or separation. The question here is – how do you guard against the dying passion and fires of romance?

Is there is something about marriages that seems to kill romantic motivation and creativity? At some point in their marriages, couples realize that they no longer take each other to feel the passion, desire, and romance that they once did. In this case, the engagement period sounds like the exciting first chapter to a rather dull book. But it does not have to be this way!

There are ways you can re-introduce, utilize, and sustain romance within a married setting. Here are some of the ways to keep the excitement, passion, and heat of love alive within your marriage. This way, it will nourish your relationship with the emotional and physical satisfaction required to you and your spouse happy.

## Romance ought to be part of your daily diet

The concept of love, especially in marriage, refers to the unconditional love and robust commitment of the partners to their partners. Romance is essential in a marriage because it is the daily manifestation of this love towards your partner. Romance is the fuel that keeps the marriage engine running. If it dies down, then everything else comes tumbling down.

Keeping romance in your daily diet means deliberately resolving to do romantic things or actions for your partner. Complement her good looks. For example, for the husband, notice how good she looks, her good mood, how good she smells, and how she makes you feel. Tell her how much you love and desire her body, and how crazy she makes you feel.

Visualizing her and letting her know about how you feel allows her to feel appreciated. It also lets her in on your thoughts, affection, love, appreciation, and attachment to her. It helps keep the romance levels high and maintain the connection you have into the marriage period.

Partners are typically good friends. However, there is a part of your relationship that goes beyond friendship. You share a marriage bed, dreams, and thoughts that are shared with no one else in the world. Therefore, making romance part of your daily interactions helps keep it alive.

This approach also develops it into a good habit to appreciate your partner every day with the same vigor and passion you did before you got married. Such a decision helps marriage through more difficult, challenging, and disruptive circumstances. For example, after the birth of your first child, the relationship and romance might be eclipsed by the attention given to the child and the accompanying chores.

However, making a deliberate effort to focus on your romance at least once a day gives you a fighting chance of maintaining your excitement, passion, and vigor even after transformative events in your lives and relationship.

## Aspire and actively seek to meet your partner's romantic needs

Part of your skillset and repertoire should be the ability to learn quickly about your spouse. Within marriages, it means continually learning about your partner through the years and adjusting your approach to suit the moments, circumstances, and periods of your life together. You become a student of your partner to answer the following question – what pleases your partner?

The learning aspect is interesting in marriage because of the gender divide in the perception of romance. Men and women view romance in different lenses. This means that you cannot use your own experience and perspective of passion for making decisions about your partner. Instead, you have to invest time and intimate conversations to establish what works and does not work for your partner.

Honesty plays a crucial role in the learning process. There is a need to be open with your partner regarding your romantic preferences. Feedback is essential to allow your partner to determine whether you like their advances or not. Such frank communications help in building an understanding of each other, which helps bolster the romantic experience for both partners in the marriage.

For example, most men find their romance in physical intimacy. For example, it matters that the female partner "dresses in a sexy way" or "meet me at the door scantily dressed." On the other hand, women typically prefer "to be taken out to a romantic candle-lit restaurant." Others prefer "cuddling in front of the fire" or "spend time talking."

The summation here is that the romantic sense for men is wired to appreciate sight and touch, whereas women want to develop a relationship.

However, meeting your spouse's romantic needs takes more than an understanding of the generic male/female taste differences. It takes a lot more work and focuses on figuring out the specific preferences, needs, wants, and expectations for your partner. When you figure this out, you will be well-positioned to meet your partner's romantic expectations and desires.

## Prioritize romance in your relationship

Romance should form a part of the most important and valuable aspects of your schedule. For example, sit down with your spouse and look at your calendars over the next week or two. Find a convenient time for both of you to go out.

Make sure you both write the data down. This will help in building the anticipation towards your day out. The building excitement drives healthy emotions for your relationship and romance.

Moreover, make sure to find time in your calendar for physical intimacy and sex. Typical married couples find no time for sex. When it comes to sex, you should aim for quantity over quality. Without having sex or intimate physical contact regularly, the risk of losing physical connection increases substantially.

The underlying argument supporting the aim for quantity and not quality is that it removes massive expectations for long and technical sessions for lovemaking. Be spontaneous. You can have a quickie in the shower. Or, you can make out like teenagers before you go to bed. The frequency of lovemaking will help build intimate moments that keep the romance alive. And, this can turn into longer lovemaking sessions to everyone's satisfaction.

## How you spend your free time matters

Every single day, make a point of spending some quality time with your partner.

How you spend your time contributes significantly towards making you a good husband/wife. You can never be too busy for your partner. Steal a moment or two to check in on him/her, say hello, and whisper sweet nothings into his ear.

Yes, you have to work, and yes, you have other things to do. However, your marriage should never be in the backburner. It should always be at the forefront of what you do.

The mistake most couples do is compartmentalize marriage and romance out of their workplace and workdays. The problem with this approach is that you spend most of the time at work. With marriage removed from the workplace, the time dedicated to your spouse reduces markedly. This makes it harder to maintain the fire of romance when it only makes technical appearances on weekends!

And if your work has to have your absolute attention, find alternative ways of making your partner feel wanted, loved, prioritized, and desired. In this regard, the less time you have available to spend with your partner, the more precious it should be when you are together.

Additionally, when pressed for time, you should make every small moment you have into a pivotal romantic experience. Obviously, your marriage will not be like your honeymoon a couple of years after you tied the knot. However, this does not mean that it should be short of mind-bending and genuinely unique moments.

As a married couple, there is a need to learn to make ostensibly small and mundane events or moments into special ones. Moments can be a small as listening to your partner intently and offering your input or help.

**Be creative**

You should turn your bedroom into a secure, private, erotic, romantic hideaway. It should not be the site for your kids to play, storage for other staff, or a workstation.

Being in the bedroom together should carry an aura of romance, building the sexual tension, heightening the desire and anticipation, and thus keeping heightening the fires of romance.

When your partner calls you and tells you, "I am in the bedroom," it should spark emotions in you connected to your shared time there as well as sexual anticipation.

Creativity also touches on communicating love and commitment to your partner. Communication is essential to the passing of information from one entity to another party. But in marriage, it takes up a new meaning.

Communicating love is not similar to how you offer a counter-offer to a client. It should be considered and steeped in the history of the relationship you share. It should also be reflective of your knowledge of your partner and nod to the love and romance you share and wish to share in the future.

Communication of love and commitment can involve something as mundane as sitting next to each other at restaurant tables. Taking a seat across from your partner is regarded as more aggressive. This is what you do when you are meeting a potential employer/employee for interviews. Sitting alongside each other allows for some erotic and romantic moments of touch and contact. You can also whisper in his/her ear.

Communication shows intent and communicates

love and romance. For example, a mutually practical communication approach within a marriage will schedule room-com date nights. In these nights, each of you can let go. Immerse yourselves in the romance, love, and relationship you share. Moreover, ensure to avoid all the externalities like work or even family. It allows you to escape together and share special moments that are important in keeping your love, passion, and romance alive.

## Turn all the positive things in your life into foreplay

Most couples focus on doing the splashy and big things to create memories and special moments in their marriages to keep their romance going. Although this approach works, it is essential to note that romance is crucially built by the small everyday actions and things you do for your partner.

Big splashy moments are great, but you cannot keep them going all week long. There is a need to device a relationship dynamic that appreciates each other through every interaction, communication, or exchange you have throughout the week.

There is a need to turn daily experiences such as

folding laundry, watching TV, doing dishes, or cooking together into moments to create a deeper connection with your spouse. Throughout the day, or in the moments of the day that you interact, you can open up about your goals, or simply check-in on each other.

Choose a couple of tasks or chores that you can do together during the day. Make sure that along with doing these chores, you maintain a secure connection, conversation, eye contact, and honest exchanges. Continually doing this helps retain the romantic and passionate streak within your marriage. It ensures that you are in touch with each other's emotions. And thus you know what to do to make your partner happy, excited, or smiling.

## Ensure the friendship with your partner is unconditional

It is essential to distinguish between the friendship you share with your partner (wife or husband) and the one you share with other close friends. In the latter, there are probably a few factors that can lead to the dissolution of said bond. Overall, you acknowledge some of the differences you have in approaching life and relating to others.

You may disagree with your friends on specific issues, but you maintain a love for each other nonetheless.

Although this mentality works in typical friendships, it is likely to lead to problems if it is transposed into a marriage dynamic. Married couples face issues with the kids, stress and depression, and issues with other family members. This means that there are likely to be several challenges affecting your relationship with your partner.

Placing conditions on your relationship with your partner will immediately establish an ultimatum beyond which the link does not exist. Therefore, it is vital to make your friendship and relationship unconditional. This allows you to be open-minded when interacting with your spouse, especially when working through disagreements.

The trick here is to ensure you treat your partner with unconditional support and understanding that you would expect or hope to receive from them. This mentality develops an understanding approach to the relationship based on honest communication and constant sharing of perspectives, emotions, feelings, and ideas as well.

## Always be in your partner's team

When it comes to issues putting your partner and the world, you should be in her corner. This should be the case whether you agree with her or not. It goes beyond accepting any differences you might have. You should take her side in public!

You should show demonstrable interest in being on your partner's side. Therefore, you should avoid saying or doing something that could leave your partner feeling unsupported, alone, or insignificant.

When your partner is put on the spot in a social situation, and they are feeling uncomfortable, you should stand up for them.

The friendship you share in marriage is a bond and connection that should be nurtured, nourished, and prioritized. Building this friendship is an everyday occurrence where you should take every opportunity to appreciate the relationship with your partner while reaffirming your commitment to your marriage.

Making sure you are on the same team every day establishes a platform to prioritize and develop your romance. This cultivation will develop a foundation to sustain your relationship down the road. It also creates a closer bond that prevents your marriage, friendship, and romance from drifting apart.

# Chapter 7 - Marriage and In-laws

## In-Law Relationships

In marriage, focusing on internal factors such as the relationship dynamic with your spouse, romance, passion, and excitement is fundamental. However, your marriage does not exist on an island. You have to deal with friends, family members, work-mates, peers, and in-laws. The relationship with your in-laws is a crucial one for a robust and durable marriage.

Extensive studies on the interaction between married couples and their in-laws show that this relationship has a massive bearing on the happiness, quality, and sustainability of a marriage. How you relate with your in-laws affects your relationship at home, and thus influences the odds of you staying together in the long haul.

It is important to note that the relationship between a son-in-law and a daughter-in-law are different. The differences typically emanate from the cultural wiring in society. However, these relationships are influenced by inherent cultural constructs, socio-cultural backgrounds, class, and even economic backgrounds.

Therefore, when figuring out your relationship with your in-laws, it is important to establish a platform and dynamic that work for your specific interaction and background factors that inform in going forward.

## Impact of Relationship with the In-Law on Marriage

Before you meet your partner, they have a pre-existing relationship with his/her parents that backdate your relationship. Typically, this relationship forms a massive history and even influences the character, personality, and mannerisms of your spouse. A partner, at the beginning of a relationship, walks into extensive account and interpretational dynamics.

Figuring out the relationship between your partner and their parents is a good start to inform your choices going forward. However, it is also essential to be open-minded when forming a relationship with in-laws. The dynamism and uncertainty of such relationships mean flexibility and open-mindedness is important.

Whether you end up adorning your partner's parents or you can rarely tolerate them, your marriage needs to have a relationship. Forming a rapport and a relationship dynamic of some sort with your partner's parents is likely to have a lasting impact on your romantic relationship.

A University of Michigan's Institute for Social Research conducted a study led by Terri Orbuch titled "Finding Love Again" in 1986 found that the relationship with in-laws is very important for married couples.

According to Orbuch's findings, a man with a close and effective relationship with his wife's parents faces a decrease in the risk of divorce by 20 percent. However, the women that indicated that they had a good and close relationship with the husband's parents experienced a surge in the risk of divorce by 20 percentage points.

These findings highlight the differences in the relationship dynamics to in-laws among married partners. It also underscores the different ways in which their relationship with their in-law's influences married partners. Overall, the lesson here is that in one way or another, the relationship with in-laws has a massive influence on marriages.

Moderating, developing, nurturing, and balancing a kinship with your in-laws takes an increasingly important role in making your marriage work and stay that way in the long haul.

## The Gender Difference in In-Laws Kinship

Typically, many men are accommodating to the idea of gaining new family members when they get married. Their kinship with their wife's parents is a crucial priority for many of them. In this regard, a successful relationship with in-laws often makes the husband content, happy, and feels welcome, which translates to a happy and long-lasting marriage.

In cases where this relationship (husband and in-laws) does not work, the resulting unhappiness, selfo-doubt, and feelings of rejection might have adverse effects on the marriage. This highlights Orbach's findings of a 20 percent surge in the risk of divorce in instances where the husband does not get along with his in-laws.

For men, in-laws offer a chance to have a "new" dad and mom without the history and entanglements that influence the relationship with their parents. They get to enjoy a home-cooked meal or a ballgame without feeling hassled or judged.

Moreover, the societal perception of men as providers means that, in many instances, they do not feel any interference from their in-laws. As a result, the relationship between husband and in-laws can develop stronger without feelings of intervention in their relationship or their marriage form the in-laws.

At the same time, a close connection between a husband and his wife's parents is important because it endears the wife to him. The resulting bond is essential for a marriage. It draws the partners closer, bolsters their love, trust, passion, and romance. A close relationship with a wife's parents implies, "*I value your family because I value and love you,*" which is a good message to send in a marriage.

The role of a daughter-in-law is significantly different from that of a son-in-law. Typically, women use their husband's parents as a route to influencing the husband's decision-making. For example, in-laws are important when she wants to get the husband to agree with her on some issue of child-rearing. In the process, they might form a closer bond with his parents to influence the husband on such a decision. However, this approach often infuriates the husband, although it can also be an effective way to influence decision-making at home.

However, this use of the relationship with in-laws for the wife can be problematic. It invites the in-laws into the affairs and decision-making process of the family. It is a slippery slope that becomes harder to stop once it begins. The resulting increase in the sense of access and ability to cross boundaries and meddle in the family is a surefire way to create conflict. The resulting friction cannot be restricted to between the daughter-in-law and her in-laws. Instead, it spills over into the marriage and causes the kind of disruption and disagreement that leads to divorce.

The opposite of the "interference aspect" for the husband happens for the wife. Meddling also leads to resentment, blame-games, blurry lines of engagement, and a break-down of relationships. This underscores Orbuch's findings that a closer husband-to-in-laws kinship leads to a decline of divorce risk by 20 percent while the equivalent link for the wife leads to a surge of the divorce risk by 20 percent.

Additionally, if the relationship between the wife

and the in-laws develops early in their marriage, life is even more detrimental to the marriage. It will disrupt the process of establishing a closer, unified, and strong bond with the husband. The budding relationship also affects the wife's ability to create clear boundaries for the in-laws, setting in motion a sequence of events that increase the risk of breaking up the marriage.

## Getting Along with In-Laws

The operating word in developing a good, warm, but balanced kinship with your in-laws is "civility." Consider the following example:

> Alicia and Will have been married for 15 years. Every time they visit Will's parents, Alicia does the dishes and washes the house only for her mother-in-law to re-do the dishes and re-wash the house. Alicia has always thought that her mother-in-law hates her and thinks that she is a slob that lives in filth; until she made known her feelings to her sister-in-law Stephanie. She told her, "*I know your mom hates me; she thinks I am a slob that exists in massive filth.*" Stephanie told her that her mother has been like this ever since they were children. She has a strong compulsion to have everything spotless. Therefore, she was not picking on Alicia.

You can imagine that Alicia will have a different perspective regarding her mother-in-law. Although the feeling of being judged and belittled will not go away completely, she will begin to understand her mother-in-law's behavior. And work towards establishing an understanding of the civil relationship.

The underlying question that emerges from this case focuses on the role of civility. How do you establish a civil and balanced relationship with your in-laws that bolster your marriage and romance? Here are some of the tops to follow to create a healthy, warm, and balanced relationship with your in-laws that will have a positive influence on the quality, happiness, and durability of your marriage.

### *Focus on Knowing your In-Laws*

You cannot have a relationship with a person or people you do not know. This goes double for your in-laws. A relationship with them should be based on honesty and constant communication. In this regard, communication comprises of your appreciation of and affection for your in-laws. Additionally, it includes the boundaries regarding what you deem acceptable and unacceptable.

Seek to understand their backgrounds, what they like, and what they dislike. Aim to establish their personalities and characters – this will come in handy in your interactions.

Moreover, ensure that face time meetings, conversations, and interactions are optimized. This can happen during holidays or on other days that are convenient for both of you. Make sure to spend some time with your in-laws socially from time to time. This will allow you to acquaint with them as a person. It will also allow them to learn about you, your character, and your personality as well.

For the man, it is vital to not only care for your wife's parents; you should be seen to care for them. This is important because it signals your love and care for your spouse.

Investing your time and effort to know your in-laws will help you make decisions regarding the extent to which your relationship, the inherent understanding, and the boundaries crucial to the sustainability of the relationship with your in-laws and most importantly, with your partner in marriage.

## *Know and Establish Your Limits*

Just because they are your in-laws does not mean you have to tell them everything. It also does not mean you have to agree with everything they tell you, or consult them in every issue you face or decision you make. It is crucial to set boundaries.

The relationship with your in-laws should be a two-way street. Due respect should be from all the parties involved in the kinship. This way, you can have good interactions but respect each other's limits and set boundaries.

To establish the right boundaries for your relationship, there is a need to shift your mentality. It is important not to follow the tropes found through popular media platforms such as films regarding in-laws. The reality is that the relationship you will share with your in-laws will be determined by specific dynamics influencing you, the relationship they have with their son/daughter (your partner), and even the distance involved.

Take competition from the kinship. There is no need to compete with your in-laws for the attention or love of your partner. Parental love is distinctive from romantic love. In some instances, you might be forced to inform your in-laws of this difference. If you think there is a hint of competition in your relationship with in-laws, acknowledge the problem. Encourage your partner to spend quality time with his or her parents every once in a while to diffuse some of their concerns.

Establishing boundaries also includes giving your in-laws planned regular visiting times, sync p with your partner regarding how you deal with your in-laws, provide them with time with the children, and embrace their interests. The target here is to make them feel welcome, supported, and respected. This way, it is easy for them to respect you back and adhere to your boundaries as well.

A working relationship will be healthy for your relationship, romance, and marriage as a whole. A healthy and balanced kinship with your in-laws will help both your partner and yourself to bolster your relationship and build and strong and long-lasting marriage.

### *Establish and Maintain a Careful Distance with your In-laws*

There is probably no "defined" distance between you and your in-laws. However, there is a "working" or "right" distance between you and your in-laws that will bolster the relationship, make it durable, while also enhancing the link with your partner in marriage.

For young couples, it is difficult to detach themselves from their parents. This is especially the case when parents want to continue with their instructional and authoritative role in their lives.

The solution here is to strike the right distance from your in-laws that allow you to have a relationship while preventing them from crossing boundaries and adversely affecting the marriage.

The right distance will focus on respecting the privacy both in-laws and the married couple. In this regard, parents can share their fears and concerns between themselves but not with their children. However, they should be ready to render a helping hand when requested by their adult children. However, they can also refuse to help with things or issues that are none of their business, such as the couple's private life.

The right distance will allow you (the married couple) and your in-laws to enjoy a well-defined relationship based on mutual respect and a clear understanding of each other's roles. This does not mean that you have to become an island and isolate yourself from your in-laws. Interaction is crucial.

As established above, the relationship or lack thereof can affect your relationship in one way or another. Therefore, continually working on the relationship with in-laws is crucial for the longevity and happiness of your marriage. It will take a constant effort because the relationship will keep evolving and changing with time.

### *Communicate Directly*

In dealing with your in-laws, try to avoid communicating through third parties. For example, do not ask you, partner, to speak to your mother-in-law in your stead about something she said or did that hurt your feelings. It is advisable to talk to your mother-in-law directly and in-person to sort this out.

This approach will make it easier for your in-laws to respect you. This will also help build the relationship because all involved will understand the importance of boundaries and civilities in your interactions.

If something is bothering you regarding the

conduct, behavior, or interaction you had with an in-law, it is vital to address it promptly. Although such issues might turn out to be genuine problems, there are cases where they are misunderstandings. Discussing them clarifies things immediately, and thus helps to communicate to in-laws about your position, perspectives, and perceptions.

Communication helps to clarify issues, traditions, and cultural adherence that might seem strange and even offensive at first. Getting to know your in-laws' backgrounds and culture is essential, as is their ability to learn yours. This is only possible through effective communication.

### *Display Maturity*

The relationship you have with your parents is different from the one you develop with your in-laws. You share a strong bond with your parents, and they have to love you. This is different for in-laws. You have to earn the love and respect of your in-laws and vice versa.

There is a need for you to accept that your in-laws will not follow the same rules and criteria as your parents. Think differently when establishing a relationship with them. Negotiate the small and more significant issues pertinent to your relationship with in-laws. This way, you can articulate yourself in a way that is respectful and commands respect and love in return.

The underlying driving concept here is that success in having a good and balanced relationship with your in-laws will have a positive impact on the quality and longevity of your marriage.

Moreover, try to be kind to your in-laws. This will help to bolster their positive views of you and thus enhance their respect and love for you.

# Chapter 8- Marriage and Finances

## Relationship between Finances and Marriage

Money is a central factor in the dynamics of a marriage. In many marriages, money is a common driving factor of arguments and stress.

It is a common misconception that couples have to share everything, including back accounts. However, there is a need to find a balance that works for your specific set of circumstances and the relationship you have.

Having separate bank accounts does not necessarily mean that your marriage is headed for failure. Such separation might allow you to be in control of your spending, eliminate the stresses of having a joint account, and breath a lease of freedom to the choices you make regarding spending.

Since finances can be a massive sticking point in a marriage, it is crucial to avoid making unilateral decisions in a marriage – especially regarding the money matters.

Although marriage built on romance, love, and passion that tend to bring partners together, there is a need for a certain extent of separation. You and your partner are individuals with spate and sometimes distinct characters, personalities, and emotional frameworks. Therefore, establishing a workable balance for your marriage regarding financial matters is important in bolstering a strong and long-lasting marriage.

## Financial Separation in Marriage

Steven Nock is a sociology professor at the University of Virginia. He specializes in studying marriage. He posits that the success of a marriage is based on the ability of each partner to establish individual validity. Therefore, a good marriage requires a significant separation among the partners to achieve such validity. It is crucial for the self-esteem of the individuals involved. Separation also allows individuals to establish a platform upon which to build their character and personality. This way, they can make a meaningful contribution towards the marriage.

Although being someone's partner is part of your

personality, it cannot be the only building block of your "self" concept. The need for separation is not highlighted as much as when it comes to addressing financial issues within a family. Typically, finances spell the freedom of your partner to do things. When all financial issues are synched, your partner will not have the freedom to be spontaneous or do something without being asked about it.

However, money separation is not the easiest feat to achieve in marriage. Conservations about money can easily get emotional and feel harsh or inconsiderate. This is especially the case when one of the spouses is making significantly less than they do. Separation might feel like they are not pulling their weight around the family. Therefore, it means walking a tight rope to achieve the right balance within the family that offers the right distance of separation while maintaining trust and romance in a marriage.

The ideal separation-together balance has the freedom to have a little fun with your own money while maintaining a sense of financial accountability to your partner. This way, although financial issues will be important in your relationship, they will not assume the "do-or-die" dimension importance that is likely to spell negative effects on the marriage.

## Solutions to Money Matters in Marriage

There is no one "right" approach to designing and handling financial matters in marriage. You will find what works for your relationship specifically for the specific set of circumstances you face as a couple. Although some studies and people support separation within the marriage, others advocate for full-disclosure and joint accounts.

A survey carried out by TD Banks in 2017, focusing on "Love and Money," found that 51 percent of all the married couples combine their finances. The study also found that 34 percent of the surveyed folks kept their money separate. The research also revealed that 15 percent did not share money at all. These findings underscore the diversity of approaches to managing financial matters in a relationship or marriage.

The trend of separation or not sharing money is highest among the younger generations. From the TD banks survey, 29 percent of the millennial couples below the age of 34 years did not share accounts. This highlights the generational and cultural factors influencing financial matters in marriages and relationships.

242

Here are some of the factors and aspects you need to be aware of when designing a way forward to handle finances in your marriage. Being mindful of these factors will be crucial in maintaining a strong and long-lasting marriage.

## *It is Strategically Better for your Relationship to Have Two Accounts Compared to One*

Although marriage brings you together in love and romance, it does not necessarily turn you into a monolithic unit. You and your partner will maintain distinct personalities, behavioral aspects, and characters. These differences will include spending habits, hobbies, and preferences. Therefore, establishing a single account to manage your money jointly will establish many areas of conflict that will negatively impact your marriage.

Divergent spending habits and financial priorities throw up areas of disagreement and potentially conflict. You can either fight about it or give up on what you want to do very badly. Sacrificing your priorities and preferences for your partner might also lead to a surge in resentment, which negatively affects your marriage.

If you decide to have one account, it is important to give each other significant space for the separation of preferences and priorities. Understanding the existence of differences establishes the room for differences in spending. This approach will also help reduce instances of sharp differences or conflict.

### *You do not have to choose one Approach – Do what works*

You do not have to choose between a joint account and financial separation. Succeeding in financial matters, within a marriage, does not require the adoption of the "mine," "yours," and "our" approach.

For example, each spouse can have a separate individual account while also contributing to a joint account to pay for the household bills, savings, or earmarked projects.

You have several options when it comes to managing your finances in a family. The most important thing here is for you and your partner to establish a framework of managing finances that leaves you with a stable plan for collective spending as well as sufficient space for individual spending and priorities.

This approach requires constant communication and honesty when it comes to spending and managing money. Making financial decisions together means that there is agreement and thus reduces the chances of developing resentment and frustrations that are potentially harmful to the marriage in the short- and the long-term.

## *Some Finances within a Family will be Inevitably Intertwined*

As a couple, finances will inevitably be part of the aspects you have to deal with together. In marriage, where you live together, you will inevitably handle bills together. As a result, it is important to come up with a structure in which you can manage your finances in a manner that is satisfactory to both of you while also avoiding the risk of sharp disagreements and conflict that can potentially destroy your marriage.

It is also crucial to consider other contingencies and/or eventualities. For example, when a couple has a joint account, and a spouse dies, the joint accounts give the survivor immediate and unrestricted access according to the law in the US. However, if you have different accounts, there is a need for documentation to prove that you have the right to the money. In some cases, the survivor has to go to probate before you can access the funds. In such cases, the surviving spouse massive an added struggle and stress to an already depressing situation or time.

Joint accounts also bolster honesty and transparency in a relationship. These factors are fundamental to a strong and long-lasting marriage. The TD Banks study revealed that around 13 percent of the respondents hid some aspects of their finances from their spouses. The study also showed that Millennials were the more likely to have undercover financial operations, with 30 percent of them admitting o this approach.

Secrets can include undisclosed accounts, clandestine credit cards, and undisclosed student debt. In the study, 35 percent of the respondents that admitted to having financial secrets did not intend ever to share their secrets with their spouses.

Financial dishonesty and secrets can be detrimental to a marriage, especially when they come to light. In some quarters, such deception is referred to as "financial infidelity," underscoring the seriousness it has on the status, quality, and longevity of a relationship or a marriage.

Establishing a healthy financial aspect within your marriage is crucial to have not only a free financial relationship but also a long-lasting marriage. The following are some of the tips to manage finances within a marriage. This is carried out in a manner that bolsters the bond between you and your partner. At the same time, it helps in steering you to financial stability.

*Share Your Financial Secrets*
Trading financial statements with your spouse is a statement of trust and openness. It means disclosing everything ranging from your income to your debts. You can start by summing up everything that you own and owe, assets, savings, and retirement accounts. Additionally, tally up your liabilities, including student debt, car loans, business loans, mortgages, and credit card balances.

The importance of such disclosure is that when you marry someone, you are combining assets and liabilities. For example, your spouse's debts and liabilities become your debts and liabilities when you get married.

You may want to help your partner to pay their loans or settle their debts. Even if you are unable to provide this kind of support, a heads-up is important. It is important to be in the know regarding such financial aspects. This is especially because these details affect your financial and credit ratings. For example, the liabilities, debts, or loans of your spouse will come into play if and when you decide to apply for a joint mortgage.

Having tabled everything, including your respective financial histories, it is time to start deliberating regarding where you want to go in your short-term and long-term future as a family. For example, decide whether you are happy with your housing situation, education plans and costs, insurance, healthcare, and work benefits, parental; financial support, and retirement plans as well.

*Focus on Developing and Following a Budget*
As a couple, your individual and collective spending has a direct impact on your respective finances as well as your joint finances.

It is time to start figuring out and scrutinizing how you have been managing costs from retirement contributions to ramen noodles.

Most couples, especially when both are working, prefer to split the costs down the middle. However, even you and your partner work, it does mean that you have to break 50-50.

Instead, the partner that earns more might want to take more responsibilities in the costs within the house while the other spouse covers the other monthly expenses. If you make more than your spouse, you might also want to contribute more to your retirement fund.

It is also crucial to pay attention to managing your daily fiancés. Here, you should focus on what makes both of you comfortable. For example, as discussed above, some couples find joint accounts to be applicable, preferable, and easy to manage. However, you might decide to retain your accounts while contributing towards joint accounts for expenses or the more substantial purchases.

Budget-tracking programs or applications on laptops, smartphones, or tablets can aid you in keeping track of your spending, your net worth, and income. Budgeting also allows you to visualize your spending, which encourages an increase in responsibility in expenditure. It also allows each partner to appreciate the contribution of their partner in your daily expenses, retirement contributions, and other more considerable expenses as well.

The orderly approach and structured design of such finances within a family provide certainty and clarity to the family. It also minimizes instances of financial infidelity. The overall result, therefore, is bolstering the strength and longevity of the marriage. This is achieved by eliminating any economic issues that might affect the marriage negatively.

*Evaluate your Compatibility as Investors*
As a family, you face decisions regarding investments of your surplus money, starting side-gigs, or taking risks. In this case, it is essential to establish some consistency or agreement(s). For example, your attitudes regarding money, as well as towards investing, have to be consistent.

Communication and compromise are crucial aspects in this aspect because attitudes and perspectives of investment and taking risks might differ between the partners. For example, you might be willing to take some risks in the market with a potentially high upside. However, your partner might be unwilling to buy into the fast-paced approach of investment and prefers to stick with the known and trusted paths of making income.

However, such disagreements are normal, and they do not necessarily mean that investing is a non-starter. In some instances, such differences of approaches might complement each other and making a worthwhile and effective partnership in business alongside the marriage. The way forward in such cases is maintaining honesty and openness. Perceptions and perspectives regarding the issues at hand should be established. Also, make sure that the decisions you make are collective to avoid any form of blame or resentment down the road.

Additionally, it is important to consult widely and research broadly to gain as much information regarding investing as possible. This will also help assuage the fears of risk that your spouse might be experiencing.

It is also essential to understand that whether you decide on an individual or a couple, it does not make the business risk you are taking any lesser. Business and investment is a learning process that you and your partner will have to undergo and experience overtime before it succeeds. If and when mistakes happen, avoid blaming your spouse. Instead, offer your support and learn from these mistakes for future reference.

*Update your will and other documents of legal importance*

Updating your will ensures certainty in case of a death. In this regard, your intentions and wishes are carried out as provided for in law. An updated will ensure that all your estate wishes are reflected in the will, and in the event of your demise, they will be carried out.

Documents regarding finances, insurance policies and retirement accounts will be relevant to the survivor. Updating these documents will make it easier for the survivor to benefit from them in the event of a death.

*Consult professionals regarding tax differences*
A joint filing of taxes significantly affects your finances. Therefore, it is crucial to make time to communicate with a tax professional regarding the different filing approaches and options. This will also allow you to figure out how different filing methods might affect your taxes.

It also allows you to re-evaluate your investment choices and thus to establish tax-efficient approaches you might take to save on costs.

Overall, managing finances is a crucial aspect of a marriage. Studies show that mismanaged funds within a marriage or financial infidelity might lead to a breakdown of families and divorce. Therefore, being keen on understanding your specific dynamics, relationship, and sources of income is essential in establishing the right balance in managing money. It is also crucial to determine the right balance between individual separation and joint spending for married couples. Figuring this out will increase the chances of both partners being happy, and thus bolstering a robust and long-lasting marriage.

# Chapter 9 - Redefining relationship roles

If you keenly observe conflicts between couples, what you will notice is that they often feel convoluted and layered in such a manner that they make it difficult to make sense of. However, there is often a dynamic that is easier to wrap our heads around. In some instances, you will see one partner start assuming the role of a parent while the other is seen as a child.

One thing you need to understand is that when you choose to break down this dynamic, you will shed more light on how acting in such a manner often infiltrates the relationship. It diminishes the love, attraction, and respect that your partner has for you. In this chapter, we will discuss the parental and childish behaviors that couples often take up and what you can do to change them in your marriage.

If you ask couples, most of them will tell you that they can relate to instances where their partners have become parental on them. In other words, they all of a sudden become instructive, disciplinary, and even superior when relating to their spouses. They may even tend to offer their spouses lots of advice or assistance just so that they can feel that they are caring for them or giving them direction.

The danger of taking up such roles is that one oversteps their boundaries and ends up doing too much for their partners. You may be thinking, but since when has too much been a bad thing? Well, since someone starts viewing you as being irresponsible and helpless.

When you assume the role of a parent when relating with your partner, the danger is that you will tend to be corrective. You start telling them what they need to do and what they should not be doing. What this result is frustration, defiance, and taking offense.

On the other hand, if in the relationship, you tend to be more childish, you may tend to cry, using passive-aggressive approaches and falling apart just so that you can get your way. In other words, you feel as though your partner is victimizing you and end up feeling helpless and reliant on them.

Having a childish behavior in a relationship is the last thing anyone would ever wish for. One thing you need to realize is that being in a relationship means that you are both mature individuals. None of you wants to be signed off as incompetent, inciting, and provocative towards their partner just for the sake of causing them to step up and take over. When your partner confronts you, a childish partner will easily sulk and feel hurt while the parental one will likely react in a parental manner. While it is so easy to see how one can easily get caught up on one side of the relationship roles that would trigger the other, you need to realize that this only creates a repetitive cycle that is painful.

Just like most couples get into conflict with each other, it is so hard to apportion blame because both sides have valid complaints about their spouse. The best thing you need to do in such a situation is caught on to such patterns and recognize when we are contributing to the cycle by playing out some significant part of it.

To know what our roles in the relationship are, you must know the specific behaviors that are associated with the parent-child dynamic. This will not only help us avoid engaging in roles that don't belong to us, but also help us strive to enjoy a relationship that has equality.

## Childish or submissive vs. parental or dominant

This is one of the most basic patterns that most people in marriage employ. In most cases, you will find one partner feeling so parental and need to control their spouse. On the other hand, one of the partners feels more childish and dominated.

What you need to realize is that the goal here is to achieve equality. In other words, you want your partner to value you, and they also expect the same from you. You ultimately have to value each other's individuality, autonomy, and independence.

## Passive and dependent vs. driven and compulsive

What you will note here is that the person with a childish behavior will often adopt a tendency of being passive and dependent on their partner. In other words, they are seeking their partner to direct and take care of them every time. A parental partner, on the other hand, will often push themselves and other people just so that they can achieve what they are looking for.

Often, this is done in a driven and critical

257

manner that makes then come off as controlling. The main objective of the two partners should be about being self-assertive and proactive in whatever they do. They should be focusing on their goals and thinking ahead so that they can go after their dreams.

## Defensive and angry vs. rigid and righteous

In such a case, you will find that one partner shuts off their partner's points of view, becomes defensive about it, and even punishes them for their feedback. In other words, when they are given suggestions or criticism, they counter attack their partners in a self-righteous manner. A partner in a childish mode, on the other hand, may often fall apart and lose their self-esteem when they are given honest feedback.

In such cases, both individuals must try as much as they can to remain non-defensive and open to each other's feedback. Realize that you are both adults and being in the adult-mode means that you are both curious and willing to explore the inputs that your partner gives you. You should welcome constructive criticism with open arms so that you can grow as an individual as well as in a relationship with each other.

## Irrational vs. moralistic

A partner in a child mode is often governed by their emotions, which often causes them to lose track of what is truly going on around them. They fail to realize what it is that is in their best interest. On the other hand, someone that is in a parent mode often goes too far for their spouse. Their focus is excessively rational that they fail to pay attention to their feelings. They end up being cynical, moralistic, and critical, something that ends up frustrating their partner who is emotionally charged.

One thing that you both need to realize is that there is a balance for the two of you. You can both try as much as you can to be rational while still paying attention to your emotional feelings. Ideally, being an adult means that you experience your emotions but then use your moral compass and aims to define your actions. This is what holds to the way you conduct yourself and your partner's behavior.

## Inability to formulate and pursue goals vs. Rigidity when formulating goals

When in a child mode, it can be very hard to pay attention or even unravel what it is that you want and how you would like to go about it. In other words, you end up operating like a ship that lacks a rudder. You end up struggling just so that you can find your way. On the other hand, if you are on a parental model, you may tend to approach pursuits rigidly. In other words, instead of pursuing goals and wants for what they are, you start seeing them as must-haves.

To build a strong relationship, you both have to stay in touch with your unique goals, wants, and needs. You both must try to formulate and implement goals by taking the appropriate approach and techniques that will help you achieve them.

## Domineering vs. covert negative power

When you assume the role of a parent, there is a high likelihood that you will come off as being bossy. In other instances, you may even be abusive of your powers, and intimidating to your partner by way of aggression and anger. Being childish, on the other hand, maybe manipulative of your partner while you try to play the victim in every situation.

It is important to note that one may control their spouse by just playing weak. They may pretend to fall apart just so that they get what they are looking for. What you have to realize is that these tendencies are destructive to your relationship.

Rather than choosing to assert power over your partner, it is the responsibility of the two of you to strive to have personal power that you can each have full control over. This will help you to change the habits and behaviors you might have that are destroying your relationship. If you choose to develop a strong sense of personal power, you will both feel strong and know that you can each affect your own lives individually.

When you and your partner realize that you are engaging in such patterns of behavior and roles, the best thing is not for you to start shifting and apportioning blames. Don't even think that the best option that you both have is to end the relationship. You both must externalize the problem. Quit trying to make the relationship better when you are not addressing the real problem that underlies your behaviors.

The truth is if you don't address the underlying cause for your relationship problems, which is redefining what your true roles are, the chances are that you will move on to the next relationship with the same dynamics. To break this cycle and prevent it from recurring in the future, you have to accept your behaviors. Be honest with yourself and start seeing how you can change the destructive cycle by changing your behavior as an individual first.

You have to start by showing a little compassion to yourself. You are acting childish, or parental may have arisen from trying to develop a defense mechanism so that we can adapt to survive better during our early lives. While these kinds of adaptations may have served you well during childhood, understand that they are hurting your relationship now.

Realize that when you engage in parental or childish roles when in marriage or a relationship, you are simply perpetuating a very unhealthy dynamic. However, when you start to challenge your behaviors and tendencies, you will successfully transform your relationship. Yes, you may feel anxious when you are most vulnerable, but in so doing, you create a better chance for you to achieve true love and connection with your partner.

# Chapter 10 - Divorce-proofing your marriage

Marriage comes with so many responsibilities and activities that need your attention all the time. The kids, work, business, family, spouse, friends, church, and many other things. At some point, you may start to feel tired and worn out. Each night you come home after work, you are too exhausted that the last thing in your mind is sex.

There are so much stress and pressure from around that you take home with you every evening. Each time you get home, the house needs cleaning, the laundry bin is full, and the kitchen sink is full of dirty dishes. All these things are waiting for you, and your mind is spinning that you even pass your spouse on the hallway, never long enough to have a meaningful conversation.

In most instances, you feel as though there is nothing meaningful for the two of you to talk about other than all the house chores waiting for you. This is how you start disconnecting from each other little by little. You get to a point where you forget that your spouse is there for you, and you also do not even try to draw them in.

Trust me; this is exactly how you start signing up for a divorce!

One mistake many couples make is thinking that marriage is a 50/50 thing. The truth is, it never has been and never will be. Realize that there are times when you have to pull nothing less than 100% of the relationship weight, and in other instances, your spouse does the same. Each one of us has days when we feel off. However, if you try the best that you can to offer your spouse the support that they need, you will also receive the same support when you need it.

You are not doing this out of obligation. You are simply doing it to keep the connection between you and your spouse secure and strong. Understand that a relationship is two-way traffic, you give and your spouse receives, and they also give and you receive. No relationship survives when one partner is doing all the work.

Now, let's start here by you asking yourself how long ago did you go out on a date with your spouse. This is one of the best ways you can start divorce-proofing your relationship. It is critical that you and your spouse go out of dates regularly, even if just to grab a coffee at the café down the street. This is a chance to focus on each other away from all the hustles and bustles of work.

Take a few minutes to flashback when you used to see each other in so much anticipation before you got married or during the early days of your marriage. Wasn't that amazing? You were in your best behaviors, well dressed, and desiring to show your partner the very best side of you. Do you still do the same?

It is very easy to let your guard down once you are married for some time. However, the magic spark between the two of you begins to disappear in the shuffle. It is critical that you talk to your spouse about your expectations and dreams, just like you used to when you were dating. It must have been so much fun dreaming together and imagining all the things that you would love to do together.

Getting married should not put a stop on these things. Your marriage should inspire you to do more together rather than dragging along into redundancy. Start dreaming together again and use your relationship as an opportunity to lift each other.

In some marriages, sex is a very big deal. Some couples begin to get resentful when they feel that they are not getting enough. I don't believe that sex is a very big deal when you have it regularly with your partner. However, the truth is that sex can be such a big deal that couples begin to hurt when they feel that they are not being touched enough by their spouses.

I like to think of it as not exactly the sexual act itself as it is about being close to the one you love. You already have a connection with your spouse, but sex adds to that connection making it even deeper. While life often gets in the way of things, the one thing that you should never forget is to strengthen that connection as much as you can.

One of the biggest factors that drive couples into divorce is contempt. It comes a time when the things you once loved about yourself are the things that bug you down today. What do you do? Do you roll your eyes and make sarcastic remarks at their expense? Each time that happens, you are killing your marriage little by little until it is no more.

Why is it that you find it so hard to give your husband the same kindness you give a stranger you met in a mall? Realize that once you start feeling contempt for your partner, the truth is that it is too late! The truth is that it is often too hard to come back from that. At this point, seeking marriage therapy may be the best option.

While I am not an official expert in marriage, the reason why my marriage is happy today is that my partner and I choose to work at it every single day. We are not perfect. We are very far from being perfect. But when you make up your mind and seriously choose to give it a try every day, you strengthen its foundation and make it hard to break. However, when you give up, then it means that you have already checked out.

What I would like you to understand is that marriage is an institution that you add something to it every single day. It is like putting loose change into a jar every day. It is like watering a plant every day. The more you add value to it, the richer your relationship gets. This can be something as simple as helping your wife cook dinner, sending your spouse a sweet text message, sending them their favorite flowers to their office, or even just hugging them or kissing them for no reason.

The truth is that everything does not always have to be a grand gesture. What is most important is making your partner always feel loved, special, and appreciated. Realize that your marriage can be the very best part of your life. If God has blessed you with children, they might benefit a lot if your marriage is good. Rather than feeling guilty for the time, you set aside to spend with your spouse, look at the greater good it does in keeping your family and marriage together.

Now, let's talk about divorce.

When you first got married to your spouse, did you ever plan for a divorce?

If there is anything so honest and refreshing, is that when you are getting married to your partner, none of you ever plans for divorce. All you are seeing and thinking about is the "Happily ever after" that you will share with the love of your life. It is only when you get there that you can start getting ready to handle what comes out of it.

If you ask the divorce attorneys today, they will tell you that even in law school, nobody teaches you the things that make people happy and connected to their partners in marriage. All you have is an opportunity to observe what constitutes an unhappy marriage. There are so many things that make relationships that were once connected to be irretrievable.

Because of what I have witnessed in my life, I have found ways that a couple can use to keep their relationship and marriage divorce-proof. These practices are what I have kept my marriage up and running for over two decades now.

## Tip 1 Be your spouse's cheerleader

As parents, couples, professionals, and normal people, some of the challenges that we face on an ongoing basis, there are so many voices that keep telling us how much of failures we are. Each night you sit to watch TV, so many adverts are out there to remind you how inadequate you are. The truth is that advertising has become the opposite of therapy. It reminds us that, above all else, we are not alright the way we are. Even when the advert is trying to sell sports cars, nuts, or even baby diapers, the message is always the same. It keeps telling us that something is wrong, missing, has a shortcoming, or is a failure.

Each you are positioned to serve as the voice of support and encouragement for your partner. Think of yourself as a shelter that your spouse needs when there is a storm of disparagement.

The truth is if you want to keep your marriage strong, healthy, and long-lasting, you need not squander the power that you have been given. Instead of joining all the critics out there who choose to shame and point out their partners in public, choose to feed your spouse with love, affection, and appreciation. Try not to compare your spouse to an imaginary partner that you heard your friends talking about in the salon. Quit comparing your spouse to some "perfect" man or woman you watched in your favorite romantic Tv series.

Realize that your partner needs a cheerleader. Don't we all? Even when there is nothing big to cheer at the moment, cheer them even for the small things that they do well every day, even for just picking the kids from school. Trust me, when your partner gets the taste of victory, they will start craving for me. That is how divorce becomes a non-existent word in your dictionary.

## Tip 2 Understand that no one can do it all

One of the most insane notions that our culture has made us believe is that when your partner does not meet all your needs at all times and in every aspect of your marriage, then they are failing at their job. They are failing you as their spouse. But is that the only measure you look at to know when they are good enough or not? Is that the only metric you need to look at when deciding whether or not to divorce them?

Perhaps your partner is a good co-parent, supportive listener, and excellent financial partner, but then are not a very exciting love you thought or wanted them to be. Maybe they don't share the same vacation dreams and food choices as you do. But the truth is that they are still good. You must try to resist the temptation of looking for a partner that meets 100% of your needs 100% of the time.

Take a step back and take a moment to reflect on the things that you consider to be at the top of your priority list. What is it that you consider a good match, and what do you consider to be less ideal? Understand that not every vice or virtue in your relationship is equal. Quit looking at love as a binary. Drop the idea that if your marriage is anything but perfect, then it sucks, and you have to get out of it. If you get a spouse that meets most of your needs most of the time, consider that a win.

## Tip 3 Recognize that the goal of marriage is equity and not equality

One of the most important things that you need

to bear in mind at all times is that you and your partner are in the business of building your marriage and relationship stronger every single day. No one in their right minds will tell you that the two of you will do the same things and bring the same value to the table.

You will be shocked to learn that some of the most successful marriages out there is quite the opposite. Look at your spouse; there are parts that they are weak at, but you are strong at. On others, it is quite the opposite. Here, total equality is not the goal.

From a legal standpoint, indeed, you don't owe your spouse a blow job, back rub, or a kind word of encouragement. You may think that you have to tell your spouse that the sex last night was mind-boggling, just so that you don't will crush their ego. But what is the point?

The truth is that you are not just doing it to soothe their ego, but you are choosing to be kind to the man or woman you love. It does not have to be hard to show your spouse some kindness. It should not be hard to lend them a helping hand when they need it.

The thing with marriage is that you have a million and one opportunities every single day to show even the least affection and kindness to your spouse. Your spouse is as human as you are. There are times when they are insecure, fragile, weak, or lonely, and they need you to be there for them. Not just there like any other person- to be present as the special person that decided to hold their hand and walk the journey of forever together.

If you both come home at the end of the day feeling stressed, don't try to belittle their stress by making yours feel more meaningful. In short, don't try to win the stress competition. If you feel that your need is not being met at that moment in time, things will not be better by trying to deprive your partner of their needs as well. If you are feeling awful, trying to make your spouse awful isn't going to help one bit!

Don't try to be equal by making your partner feel the same way you felt, too, when they failed to meet your needs. Realize that equality is not the goal here. It is about being fair. If they are not kind to you, choose to show them kindness instead. Let your needs take a back seat so that you can offer your spouse a good measure of kindness and selfless support like a close friend would. When you make their happiness the center of your focus, they start doing the same for you.

## Tip 4 Remember that it is possible that you could get a divorce

Most couples don't like talking about divorce. However, you need to realize that pretending that you never fall ill does not mean that you will remain healthy at all times. Trying not to think about funerals does not mean that you are immortal.

If there is one fastest way you can ruin your marriage is to think that the mere fact that divorce never comes up in your conversations means that you will never have to. When you stay open to talking about divorce with your partner, you give each other a chance to put into perspective all severe your connection will be hurt if your marriage ends.

When you hear someone died, you quickly become aware of how lucky you are to have the gift of love. When you go see a friend admitted to the hospital, you start to see the value of being healthy.

In the same way, when you walked down the aisle, the love of your spouse was not permanent and irrevocable. It was a gift. It was something that you were loaned. This means that you have to proceed accordingly. Always think of divorce to get the perspective of how lucky you are to have your spouse and how fragile you need to start treating your relationship with them.

Remember, you had all it took to fall in love. You also have all it takes to stay in the marriage.

The choice is yours!

**One last word**

Every marriage and relationship have their highs and lows. The most important thing is to take note of your actions. Ask yourself whether you are contributing to the weakening of your connection with your spouse. Ask yourself whether you are doing everything in your power to be the best partner to your spouse. Are you failing in some areas? Is there something that you can do to improve your relationship?

Some of the subtle habits we have often are harmful to our relationships, and they stand in the way of you enjoying a "happily ever after" that you promised your spouse at the altar. God designed the institution of marriage to last forever, and he has specifically given us the instructions that help us gain happiness and peace in the marriage.

You will note that most marriages break because of personal problems; self-centeredness, irresponsibility, and competition. These things threaten the very foundation of marriage. What you need to understand is that the will of God was for you and your spouse to enjoy a marriage that is characterized by sacrifice, commitment, love, and cooperation. That is what a healthy marriage is all about.

There are times when you feel like giving up your marriage because of trying and feeling like there is no change. One thing you need to realize is that there is no upset too big that you end up abandoning your commitment and all the efforts that you have invested in your marriage. You have both come a long way just to throw away your marriage like that.

You have the power to make your marriage strong, healthy, and long-lasting. You have the blessings and support from God to take you through each day together. When you choose to be loyal and hold each other's hands every step of the way, you will not only achieve mutual enjoyment, but you will establish a solid connection that no annoyance can break it down.

So, what are you still waiting for?

Start taking control of your marriage and work at nothing but establishing a strong, healthy, and long-lasting relationship with your spouse.

You can do it! Best Wishes.

© **written by: Katerina Griffith**

slowly laid the rifle across her lap. She felt for her cigarettes, lit one with trembling fingers, inhaled deep.

Now, think this through, Johnson . . . there are no such things as fiends and goblins. *You're safer here than in the streets of New York . . .*

Then the doorway darkened as a dreadful fiend blocked out the light; her eyes widened in terror, a scream welled up, and she grabbed up the gun.

Smoky bear stared at her a petrified instant, then he whirled about and plunged out of the doorway.

He bounded off the porch and went galloping into the undergrowth, and Elizabeth yelled, 'Smoky! . . .'

He blundered on into the trees; then stopped when he heard his name. Flanks heaving, he looked back fearfully over his shoulder.

'Oh clever Smoky! How did you *find* us?' Her heart was still hammering.

She could just see him in the shadows. But she had seen his limp.

'Poor Smoky. What's happened to you?' It was like seeing an old friend—and she wasn't alone anymore. 'Come here, Smoky. Come . . .'

Smoky stood, listening to her reassuring voice, wanting to trust her, but not daring to. He remembered her from the first day in the glen: he could smell the other animals; he knew his keeper must be near, and he was too sore to run any farther.

Elizabeth withdrew from the window, and reached for her medical bag. Perhaps it was crazy, but she was going to do it: she was about to approach a wounded animal four times her size and try to treat him—alone. Without iron bars, straitjackets, assistants. In the zoo she would have half a dozen people helping her. Her heart was hammering again. But she knew, without hesitation, that she was going to do her duty: this was what she was here for.

She pulled out the tranquilizer pistol, and shakily slotted in a cartridge. She took a deep breath and stepped slowly through the doorway.

'Hello, Smoky,' she smiled.

268

warned her, loud and clear, last night, that he wanted her out. And if he was just taking the animals out, why had he taken his sleeping bag? He obviously didn't intend returning tonight. He had left her the gun, for protection. He did not need the gun because he wasn't going to feed the lions again—and Charlie had one of the sheriff's guns.

The panic surged back—she felt the eerie fear of discovering herself completely alone. Of the ringing quiet of the wilderness, as if everything was watching her. The primeval menace of it. And Elizabeth wanted the rifle. She dashed back to the cabin. She picked up the gun, her eyes darting from the window to the door. She sidled into the corner; then looked at the gun in her shaking hands. Was it loaded? No—Davey would never leave a loaded gun around. How did it work? She was looking at a simple Winchester, with a silencer and telescopic sights. She identified the bolt action, and pulled it open recklessly, half expecting the thing to explode. It opened with a business-like click. The chamber was empty.

She looked for the cartridges, found a small box. She hastily slid one into the chamber and closed the bolt.

The thing was ready to fire . . .

And, definitely, she felt safer with the gun in her hands. And, suddenly, she also felt foolish.

What was the gun going to protect her against? From hillbilly murderers? From Sheriff Lonnogan and his posse?

She took a deep, quivering breath.

No, realistically, she was not afraid of them. It was the very wilderness she was afraid of. Like that first night in her rented car in the mountains outside Erwin. The primitive fear of the forest, the dark unknown, the *menace* of goblins and demons, dreadful fiends and evil spirits, lurking in low places. More than anything else she wanted to run for her life until she burst out of menacing low-lying darkness into the sunlit high places. O God, God, how thin the veneer of civilization . . . And, oh, she understood the human need for the cave, to gird ourselves against fearsome Nature—and for woman to cling unto man. By God she wanted Davey Jordan around now.

She made her muscles untense. She made herself sit down. She

267

yesterday. 'Things are going to start happening.' 'Do you know your way out of here?' And now, because she had refused, he had just left her to it. She looked feverishly around again, for a note, perhaps.

But there was nothing.

Panic. She pulled on her sweater, jeans, sneakers. Then she rolled up her sleeping bag and shakily strapped it to her knapsack. Then stopped.

To go where? ...

Where was she going with her knapsack? Cherokee? To look for the animals? How was she going to find them if Davey could run rings round the experts, as he said? She stood, collecting her wits. The she dashed outside.

She crouched and examined the ground for spoor.

There was spoor everywhere. It all looked fresh. She hurried toward the pasture for twenty paces: more spoor. Elephants'. Gorillas'. Bears'. It could be today's or yesterday's

She felt helpless. What spoor to follow? She knew the only thing to do, but she had no confidence in herself doing it: 'a three-sixty.' Walk a big circle around the cabin, decide on the freshest spoor, and follow it. That was the scientific way she had learned on zoological expeditions, but she had not been good. She would follow the wrong spoor. How would she even *see* the spoor in that shadowed forest? She could get hopelessly lost. *Lost* ... Then came the primitive fear of being alone in the dark wilderness. *Pull yourself together. There is nothing to be afraid of. You are not lost yet. You know how to get out of here.* Now, *think* ...

Why did she assume that Davey had just abandoned her? Or Charlie? He had said he was going to split up the animals—that was what he was doing, just taking the animals out, to resettle them. Would Davey be so cruel as to leave her alone in the wilderness after all she had done for him? Or Big Charlie? ...

She closed her eyes. The answer was yes.

A man who had the audacity to rob a zoo and a circus to return his beloved animals to the wild was just the sort of man to abandon you if it became necessary. All he cared about was those animals. And what *had* she done for him? Nothing but try to argue him out of it. She had not even had to use her medical skills yet. And he had

266

to swat him, good luck. Otherwise it's unfair; one of us gets the best trophy and the other two just got to watch him have the fun.'

'Supposing we all see him at the same time?'

'Fine. We all have a crack at him.'

'And the skin?'

'In that case we dice for the skin, like we did for this bitch.' He jerked his head at Mama. 'Same deal with the wolf.'

'We should try to knock that wolf off first of all,' the first man said. 'He'll make trouble.'

'Sure. Get the bastard out of the way.' He added, with a smirk, 'Be kind of good to get that Indian and Jordan out the way too . . .'

They all smiled. 'Wouldn't that be something?'

The second man thought, then said, 'Say, you know where I reckon we should go next year? Brazil.'

'Why the hell Brazil?'

'Because,' the second man said, 'I hear it's about the last place left where you can bag yourself a real live Indian.'

# forty-nine

At sunrise, Elizabeth was suddenly wide awake.

She lay in her sleeping bag, tensed, listening. There was complete silence. Then she realized that was what it was: the silence. Suddenly she knew, with awful certainty, that she was alone.

She scrambled out of her sleeping bag, wearing only her bra and panties, dashed to the door of the cabin and looked out. Her heart sank. She stared into the wilderness morning: they were gone.

There was not a sign of anybody. The porch, where Big Charlie and Davey slept, was empty. Their bedrolls and knapsacks were gone. There was not an animal in sight. She felt the panic rising. She spun around, and her eyes darted about the cabin. All that remained was their rifle and their stewing pot.

She stood there, her mind fumbling over what he had said